Awake Parenting
Parenting with Purpose,
Presence and Power

Scott Mills, Ph.D.
with Dan Kaufman, Ed.D.

ISBN 978-0-578-02363-2

Cover art designed by James Hummel.

www.velvetyak.com

This book is dedicated to my amazing family who has loved me, challenged me, nurtured me and taught me what it means to be a compassionate, loving human being in a chaotic world. Especially for my mother Lise, whose expansive heart constantly inspires and whose sense of humor keeps me in stitches, my amazing grandparents, and all the people who have loved, taught, inspired and supported me, including my clients, in this amazing project!

Scott Mills, Ph.D.

This book is dedicated to my own parents who, unknowingly and unwittingly, taught me about compassion and to all the many families and youth that I have worked with over the years who have taught me about love, courage and humility.

Dan Kaufman, Ed.D.

Table of Contents

PART IV: POWER

Note to the Reader

We have made some style choices in order to make things really clear for readers. Since there are two of us writing we wanted you to be able tell us apart. Scott is the primary author and so if you see "I" it means just him. If you see Dan, it refers to Dan. And if you see "we," it's both of us.

We also wanted to make sure that, just like in our coaching practices, men and women had an equal voice. We don't have a great gender-neutral pronoun in English yet so we decided to follow a trend that has become popular the last fifteen or twenty years. We have used "they" and "them" in place of "he, she, him and her." It may take a few pages to get used to but it will quickly fade into to the background. It seems to us like a small price to pay for everyone to feel included.

Introduction

"It's not only children who grow. Parents do too. As much as we watch to see what our children do with their lives, they are watching us to see what we do with ours. I can't tell my children to reach for the sun. All I can do is reach for it, myself."

~ *Joyce Maynard, American author*

The other day I was at a concert when a woman who I hadn't seen in a while struck up a conversation with me. She wanted to know what I had been up to lately and, of course, I couldn't help but tell her about the amazing work that Dan and I have been doing to support parents and families all over the country. As I watched her shoulders rise and her face tighten, I knew I had struck a nerve. "It's easy to offer advice when you aren't in the middle of craziness with your kid. But sometimes I just want to shake them to stop them doing what they are doing!" The frustration in her voice made it clear that she, like so many parents we work with, are simply feeling at their wit's end.

Welcome to the journey we affectionately call **awake parenting**. We wrote it for all you parents and people who work with children who want something more in your relationships with the children in your life. Wherever you are in your life, no matter the age of your children, you've found yourself with this book in your hands. You might be hoping to find ways to protect your children or to build a stronger relationship. You are likely experiencing the impact of our rapidly changing world, feeling stressed out and looking for answers. And you might even feel a bit conflicted. One part of you may believe that your situation is unique, unchangeable or even hopeless. And then there's the part of you that is longing for change and knows that the practices we will offer have worked for people just like you. We aren't asking you to believe that simply reading this book will change your relationship with your children. But we do believe that small changes can make a big difference. Just by picking up this book and reading it, you are offering yourself a whole new set of possibilities. We are honored that you are allowing yourself to be guided by us in this process.

Everyday Dan and I work with children and families seeking change in their lives. Many of our clients come to us during very difficult periods in their lives. Dan spends much of his time helping families dealing with substance abuse move into a place of strength and hope, rebuilding fractured family systems so they are better for the journey. I came to coaching after working for years with children and families living in extreme poverty and dealing with life threatening illnesses like HIV/AIDS assisting them in building life skills and moving boldly forward into hope. Regardless of whether our clients have been rich or poor, struggling to wake up in the morning or looking for new ways to excel, have already tried lots of things or are just beginning down a path of wholeness, we have seen the approaches we offer in this book change lives.

The work that we offer is a unique approach to coaching. It began a few years ago when Dan and I began to collaborate on ways to bring together the best tools and techniques across a wide variety of disciplines to support our clients. Together we brought Eastern and Western psychology, spirituality, art, drama, music and meditation to the table. We mixed hypnosis, visualization and neuro-linguistic programming into the stew. And we continue to explore new paths that assist clients in stepping powerfully and quickly into the lives they desire. With such a vast array of tools and experiences at our disposal, we have facilitated powerful transformation in our clients. While there is no substitute for working one-on-one with a coach who can custom tailor a process just for you, we offer much of what we have used with our clients over the years in this book.

Who is this book for?

This book is written for parents just like you. Parents who are worried about how to best raise their children. Parents who are worried that their children will get into drugs or gangs, worried that their kids will run away, worried that they are having sex, and worried that they will be unprepared for our chaotic world.

Most of the parents we talk to lately are overstressed, worn out and confused. They want to be the best parents they can be, yet economic chaos and life seem too often to get in the way. They are literally feeling pulled apart by the competing demands of work, family, self and community. The world is changing fast and parents are often uncertain how to take care of themselves much less their children.

We hear questions like, "What is the best way for my children to use the Internet? Are there predators out to get them online? Where are they safe? How do I keep my kids away from drugs and alcohol? Are they having sex? Are they being safe?"

Parents of very young children are asking if the food their children are eating is healthy or loaded with chemicals that will later cause illness or obesity. Are the toys they are playing with filled with lead and other toxins? We have written this book for parents with these types of questions.

It is also written for parents who have big dreams for their children. Who want to support them in creating amazing success, love and happiness in their lives. Who are eager to watch them grow into strong, compassionate adults who are living their dreams.

Most parents have both sets of questions in mind. We hear parents asking us, "How can I help my child do better in school? How can I support them in being confident and independent and still let them know I am there for them? How can I help them make choices about the big decisions that they face in life?"

Finally, we wrote this book for parents who want to feel good about themselves. Who want to live their own dreams, expand their lives, laugh more and invite boundless joy into their hearts. Are asking questions like, "How can I balance my desires with the needs of my children? How can I make sure my partnership stays strong in the midst of the demands of parenting? How can I not take myself so seriously and have more fun?"

If you find yourself asking any of these questions, we are happy you have found your way to this book. You have a powerful tool in your hands for addressing many of your questions and discovering powerful new ways to move forward in your life.

Pebbles in the Pond

The mother I told you about in the beginning of this chapter, like many of the frustrated mothers we frequently encounter, was feeling a lost. She needed something that she hadn't yet put her finger on. Knowing I had only a few minutes before the intermission was over and Joan Baez would return to the stage, I dove in. I took a deep look at her, acknowledged all the frustration that she must be feeling in that moment, and asked her what she really wanted for herself and her children. As she told me a few of her hopes her face softened and her whole body relaxed. Then I asked her, "What is the one thing that you could ask for in this moment that would move you towards your longing?" She paused as she considered my question and said, " I could really use a hug right now."

As I extended my arms, I could feel her let go just a little and breathe just a little deeper. She arrived a bit more fully in that moment. And once again it became clear to me how a small action in the moment can create a momentary shift. Repeated small actions can create global change. Waking up rarely happens all at once. It's a series of small steps that taken one at a time add up to bring change into our lives.

Each step along this path is a step towards waking up to fuller lives for you and your children. Like a pebble dropped into a pond, even small changes can have a profound impact on your life. Each time you make a new choice, each time you practice a new behavior and each time you think a new thought you will be building an unstoppable momentum towards aliveness, passion and deeper relationship. And the tools that you learn in this book will transcend your family. They offer the possibility of more space and movement in your work, your friendships, and even your love life. Once you wake up in one area of your life, somehow sleep walking in the others just isn't as easy anymore.

One of the most powerful ways we teach children to live awake lives is by being awake ourselves. Being around other people who are full of life is simply contagious. When parents are vital, loving, awake human beings then children see that path is available to them as well. When parents are sleep walking through life, it's much harder to heed their counsel about things like drugs and alcohol. If what you're doing in your life isn't really working to make you happy, your

9

children will see that and question all you offer. Don't you prefer to follow people who are living examples of what they teach?

So this work is really about coming into relationship with yourself and your children at the same time. It takes some courage, as all genuine change does, to realize that the most important way that you can shift your family dynamics and help your children navigate the perils of our world is to live as an example.

Points of Departure

There are some basic ideas that we believe are mostly true on this journey towards waking up. You will see them come up throughout the book. You don't have to agree with them but we invite you to try them on while you read. Just see how they fit. If they don't, when you finish the book just leave them where you found them. You might find yourself surprised at how much easier relating can be when you have a more gentle perspective.

You've been doing the best you can.

No matter what actions you have taken in the past, no matter what you have said that has been hurtful, no matter what decisions that you have made that you would now change, everything you have done in your life has been with a higher intention. You have been working to fulfill your needs. Sometimes, maybe even often, you haven't been as skillful as you would have liked to be. If you can allow yourself to recognize that you have done what you've done with the goal of meeting your needs, you can release the guilt and pain of the past and make new choices now. Based on this understanding, your new choices will lead you to deeper relationships in more skillful ways.

The deepest changes come at the subconscious level.

Sometimes we put out lots of effort and don't see the results we would like. I believe this is because we are using the smallest oar in the boat to try to steer. Our conscious decisions can be powerful impetus to create change. When you decide to read a book or listen to a hypnosis tape or go to a seminar you are making conscious choices to change. Making a conscious choice for change can set it all in motion. But once it's there the subconscious mind can guide the boat. Imagine that the subconscious is the operating system of your computer and the conscious are the files on your desktop. Reorganizing the desktop can make life easier but changing the operating system affects global change. In this book, we will work with both, allowing the subconscious mind to find new images, metaphors and language to support your conscious mind in making the change you want.

You have all the resources you need.

You have done a pretty good job in your life so far, probably better than you give yourself credit for. And while many of us believe the answer to our problems is outside ourselves, we invite you to notice how resourceful you actually are. Think of all of the problems you have solved in your life, the things that you have learned and the obstacles that you have overcome. Allow these resources to be your guide as you add new options throughout this book. You are capable of making the changes in your life that you would like and you have all the resources you need to get there within your reach.

The parenting journey is a spiritual one.

Regardless of your journey in life, if you have held a baby in your arms, you know that there is something bigger than yourself in this world. You know that there has to be more than simply acquiring more and being comfortable. We believe this is a call of spirit, a call to be something greater than we are. Life shows up in ways to help us learn to wake up, to connect with something larger than ourselves, open our hearts and heal the wounds of the world. No matter which path you might be on, or if you are on no particular path, we invite you to notice what life might be asking from you on your journey, to notice the profound ways that you are being called to connect to yourself, your children and the others all around you everyday.

The more flexible you can be the easier life will be.

The oldest trees have deep roots. Their groundedness allows them to sway with very strong winds, to be flexible and stand their ground. The more grounded you are the more options will be available to you. In this work our goal is to assist you in gaining more options and flexibility. The more colors in your palette, the more possibilities for your canvas. The more keys on your piano, the more possibilities for newness in your music. Just because you learn a new note you don't leave the old ones behind. So allow yourself to imagine all the ways that you can incorporate the new tools we will teach you. Imagine how they can be used with the old tools you have and where the new tools are more useful for you.

Practice makes plenty.

We don't want you to forget about perfection. Some day that may come in handy if you are fixing a car or building furniture from Ikea. But in relationships, there is no perfection. The more that you practice the tools and perspectives that we offer, the more you will experience more fullness, more life, and more vitality in your relationships. So allow yourself to practice with compassion and gentleness knowing that each step you take is like a pebble dropped into the water. It will reverberate out into places that you don't yet know.

How to Use this Book

Our intention in offering this book to you is to support as much practical, concrete change in your life as you want. We know that you will be motivated to move forward as you see results emerging from the practices. In this simple guidebook we've explained seven major foundations of awake parenting as well as the tools to incorporate them into your life. Throughout this book we introduce you to these concepts in short chapters that give you useful ways to support you in creating the relationship you want with your children. The more you practice, the more you will get out of the work. Every chapter and its accompanying practices are designed with busy parents in mind. They don't take long to read and the practices can be done without disrupting your day.

We suggest you read the basic principles first to plant them firmly in your mind. All of the practices we provide grow from these seven simple, very important ideas. From there, start wherever you like. You can wake up anywhere. You can practice more awake parenting anytime. Just as it doesn't matter where you drop a pebble in a pond, you will see ripples move out from the center. The same is true of these practices. No matter where you start they can lead you to greater awareness and deeper relationship with yourself, your partner and your children.

Invitation

We are so pleased that you have chosen to read this book. As you read, we ask you to keep the end goal in mind. Take a minute and imagine what that might be. What kind of relationships might you imagine for yourself and your children? Let that take full form in your mind knowing what it feels like in your body to have that kind of relationship, what the sounds you might hear are, perhaps your happy children laughing, and finally what it would look like to have that kind of relationship. Know that with each practice and observation you engage, you will be moving closer and closer to this goal.

PART I: FOUNDATIONS OF AWAKE PARENTING

Chapter 2: A Call to Awake Parenting

Don't worry that children never listen to you; worry that they are always watching you. ~Robert Fulghum

To bring up a child in the way he should go, travel that way yourself once in a while. ~Josh Billings

I like to take road trips. When I was younger I would often set off on road trips with only my dog, a map, some CDs and a few bucks to see what I could find. As long as I knew my general direction, the maps were really useful in helping me to get where I was going. But in the days before GPS, there were times when the maps failed me. They wouldn't know that there was road construction for 40 miles on the small off-highway route I had chosen or that a road had been closed. And I was left on my own to find another route.

Our way of understanding the world is a form of mapping. We know that there are certain actions that we can take to get us from one place to another. And there are words that when said at the right time can get us just what we want. Parents have maps like this that tell them the best way to parent their children. Sometimes the maps are old and dusty. They may have been inherited from earlier generations or from culture. And they may lead us to closed roads or disaster zones.

Chances are you know a bit about your maps but until you start to really pay attention to them, they function in the background on autopilot. The more that you pay attention to the choices that you make and why you make them, the more capable you will become in making new choices. We have many, many beliefs and patterns of behavior that come from our childhood. Until we take them out, shake off the dust and hold them up to the light, it's hard to decide if they are really serving us or are just so familiar that we no longer even notice them. Until we have chosen them ourselves, we haven't really made them our own. We have just inherited them from our parents. Can you imagine if you inherited your entire wardrobe from your parents? There are certainly items that you would love and wear with pride.

There are also others that wouldn't fit you and you would let go.

We want to offer you a new map to navigate the world of parenting. It's one that you can overlay onto your own and see what fits with your experience. There are seven great pathways or principles that we identify on this map. These are the foundational principles of awake parenting and are drawn from our work with clients, our research and our own lives. We invite you to try these on and see how they might fit in your life. We will explain them briefly in this chapter and then offer much greater detail in the chapters that follow.

The seven basic pathways or guidelines for awake parenting that we will build on throughout this work are rooted in the best of psychology as well as spiritual traditions from around the world. You do not have to have any particular spiritual path for these principles to work for you. We have seen them work with people of faith, people who are agnostic and people of no faith. It does help if you can try on the seven principles temporarily to see how they work. If you are looking for a reason that they are not true, then it will be much harder for you to experience success. By all means enter with a critical mind and at the same time give yourself permission to try on new ideas that might be different than what you are used to. You can always come back to do what you've always done and get the results you have always gotten.

Sometimes people can react to one of these principles strongly. Those things that you most forcefully respond to may hold the most potential for growth for you. There may be something in the principle that challenges the basic story that you are telling about yourself or the way that you understand who you are. Our goal isn't to be right or to make you wrong. If you have a response like that we simply suggest that you dig into it a little deeper. Ask yourself what's at the bottom of that reaction. Does it challenge your previous experience? Does it challenge or even contradict one of your core beliefs? Where does it come from? Is it serving you well? Please keep anything that is serving you and your family well. Only you can know what the consequences of your beliefs are for your family.

The Seven Pathways of Awake Parenting

Pathway 1: Owning Your Own Choices

Are you the captain of your ship making decisions for where it goes or are you a deck hand simply taking orders, swabbing the deck and cleaning up when other people get seasick? As a parent you know a lot about being in command of the lives of others. You have no choice but to be responsible for the wellbeing of your children.

Are you also taking full responsibility for your experience? Do you realize how much power you really have? Most people have far more power than they take credit for. You give away your power each time you assume that other people are causing you to feel or act some way. We believe you can choose to act and feel anyway that you want. We'll explain how this works in Chapter 3.

Pathway 2: Cultivating Awareness

When we are only partially aware of what's going on, we only make partially sane choices. If you listen with your head but not your heart, you only have part of the information that you need. In our fast paced world, slowing down enough to be present to the lives of your children and to hearing what they are really saying is one of the greatest leverage points for shifting your relationship with your kids. Chapter 4 will show you how you can find moments of stillness that can feed your soul and create a stronger foundation for your relationships.

Pathway 3: Practicing Gratitude

Ever notice you tend to find only what you are looking for? If you are looking for a knife in the kitchen drawer, you will generally not see all the spoons. The same is true of the way you experience people. When you are watching just to make sure your kids stay out of trouble, it's easy to get pretty focused on trouble. That means that your primary partner in relationship is conflict. There is no doubt that kids will make mistakes in the process of learning to be all grown up (we are still in that process ourselves, aren't we?) and boundaries will have to be set and consequences applied to poor choices. However, relating to anyone primarily through conflict is exhausting. In Chapter

5, we suggest that a more effective way of relating is through gratitude, allowing you to see all of who your children are no matter the circumstances.

Pathway 4: Living in Abundance

A few nights ago, I dreamed that I was in an amazing orchard filled with every kind of fruit tree that you can imagine. It was brimming over with life and ripe fruit. But it required me to look up to see the fullness of the branches and all they were offering, to expand my normal range of vision to see how available all of this was, free for the picking. It can be easy to fall into a "scarcity mentality" that teaches your children that the world is hard, scary and full of danger. One of the greatest gifts you can give your children is to practice an abundance mentality where you don't ignore the dangers of the world but instead hold them in balance with all that life has to offer. In Chapter 6, we suggest how you might see what's shaking on the branches hanging over your head.

Pathway 5: Releasing Expectations

Ever feel like no matter what you did, you just couldn't please someone in your life? Chances are you were suffering from expectation sickness, the dreaded disease where others have expectations for you that don't fit into your deepest sense of purpose. They don't reflect who you are. It's often easy to see this is in romantic relationships. Do you expect the man to hold open the door or pull out your chair? Do you expect the woman to pay for dinner? Do you expect that your date will call you within a certain amount of time after the date? We all hold these unwritten rules. It would probably be easier if we could just pass them out at the beginning of a new relationship. Perhaps on a note card that says, "Here are my expectations of you as my friend, lover, child, etc. Violate them at your own risk." In Chapter 7, we explain the suffocating affect of our expectations on others and suggest how we might see people for who they really are.

Pathway 6: Breathing Compassion

All of life is deeply interconnected. Scientists worldwide continue to find more and more ways in which small actions in one place can create changes in others. Compassion is the radical awareness of our deep interconnection with all other human beings on the planet, even those we don't like. We share connections. We breathe the same air. We depend on the same soil. We drink the same water and apparently we are all somehow related to Kevin Bacon. In Chapter 8, we suggest that if we start with this understanding of compassion, it shifts the way we think, what we say, and how we act in relationship to others. Nowhere is this truer than with our families.

Pathway 7: Practice Makes Plenty

We don't really practice being in relationship. Instead, we tell stories about who we are. I have a few of them and I bet you do too. They often begin with the words, "I am." You might tell yourself and others that you are lazy, selfish, always late, incapable of losing weight, not important enough to do something really important, impatient, easily angered. But these are just stories. They are interpretations of ourselves based on our past actions. People change all the time. In fact, you have the capacity to change anytime you want to.

The stories that we tell are descriptions of the patterns of relationship that we have been practicing in our lives. Here are some past stories that people have told about relationships in our culture that thankfully are no longer considered to be true:

- Some people should be owned by others.
- Women should stay home and have children.
- Men can't show emotions.
- Gay men and lesbians can't have children.
- White people are better than black people.
- Children should be seen but not heard.
- Rich people are better than poor people.
- Women are better than men.

- Men are better than women.

- The Earth is an object for humans to use any way we please.

- We are alone in the world. We have to look out for number one.

These are all just stories we have told. However, as soon as we changed our thinking, we started putting new practices in place that reflected new realities. Even in the last twenty years, radical shifts in our stories have occurred. With the election of President Barack Obama the final nails are being hammered into the coffin of the belief that black people are inferior. Women are C.E.O.s, lawyers, doctors and some choose to stay home and take care of their children. More and more men are showing their emotions and connecting to others. Gay men and women across the world have proven to be amazing parents. All of these changes began by telling new stories that allowed for new possibilities and were solidified with practice.

To change the stories that you have told about yourself requires that you create new paths to follow. The old ruts are comfortable and familiar. They are easy to fall back into until we have created new, more life giving paths. In Chapter 9, as well as throughout the text, we will suggest ways to make practicing being awake parents fun and engaging!

The Way Forward: Three Flows of Change

The seven pathways that we have described are avenues for us to move forward in our lives. With the assistance of Dr. Cathy Rodgers, Ph.D., I have created a model of thinking about the vital forces or energies that propel us down those paths. This way of thinking about change has given many of my clients a firmer handle on ways they can create change in their lives.

I call it the Embodied Model of Change. Since we are human beings, living systems if you will, it seemed only natural that we would develop a model of change that relates to how our bodies move, flow and change across a day as well as our lifetime. There are three major streams of change that we see when people shift their lives. We have organized this book around these streams.

Purpose

If you have ever walked into another room to get something and then completely forgotten what it was, you know what I mean when I say we have lost our purpose. Many of us simply don't know where we are heading and what our lives are about. Figuring this out, especially when it can be done within the context of the family, can move us out of a fog and into the light. We consider purpose the animating force, like breath or blood, of the body. When it is flowing smoothly, we are filled with energy, vitality and health. When it slows down or becomes stagnant we are in for trouble. All of our actions seem out of joint or lacking meaning.

The chapters that we present on purpose help to identify what you really want to create in your life. Of course, we have started with the assumption that each of you reading probably wants to be more awake, more loving parents with stronger relationships with your children. But what does that look like for you and how might you set your sails in that direction? This section will help answer those questions.

Presence

Raffle tickets often say, "Must be present to win." We believe the same is true in life. When we walk around with our heads full of thoughts of what happened this morning and what might happen tomorrow, or we are doing so many things at once that we barely notice the person in front of us, it is hard to really be present. We consider this to be the basis of structural integrity so we have likened presence to the bones. When the bones are strong, when we are fully present, we are able to support ourselves and others. We can move with ease and even run and jump. As our bones become brittle, we break easily under pressure and lose our capacity to engage in many of the significant activities that we would like to be doing.

One of the easiest ways to understand what we mean by presence is to notice the way that you show up for life. Have you ever gone to a party that you weren't sure you wanted to attend? Perhaps your mind was racing with thoughts that no one at the party would talk to you or that you would say the wrong thing and embarrass yourself. Or maybe you just had a fight with a friend and were replaying it in your head. How is that different than if you showed up to the same party with a bottle of wine, looking forward to seeing a dear friend who had been away on a long trip? The way you interact with the people at the party, the way they respond to you, the amount of fun you have and even what you remember will all be greatly impacted by how you show up to the party. And you can choose to show up in a way that will open you up to new possibility, deeper connection and greater love. The chapters in this section help you explore ways to show up more awake, alive and loving.

Power

Too many people confuse power with force. They may use forceful actions like shouting, hitting and other controlling behaviors to get their families to do what they want. The same tactics are often used in the workplace where threats are all too often commonplace. These can be useful in emergencies but as lifelong strategies for communication and growth, they fail miserably. We offer an alternative that we call power. Powerful actions strengthen everyone involved, build relationships and allow children to grow into healthy, wise adults. We liken this function to the muscles of the body that with practice can be strengthened, stretched and defined.

The section on power expand the options that you have for relating to your children. Remember when you were young and you used to get 24 Crayola crayons in a box? You drew all kinds of things with those 24 little colors. But then one day you moved up to the 64-color box and your choices took a quantum leap. Just like you didn't stop using the initial 24 colors, you don't have to give up any of the ways that you are currently relating to your children. We simply offer you more colors to choose from.

Invitation

The rest of the book is about how to apply the pathways and flows in your daily life. We designed the process of incorporating these concepts into your daily life to be a gentle process. Imagine sinking into a hot tub little by little, eventually feeling your body relax and your mind settle into bliss. The concepts are easy to grasp and the practices are simple. You can easily include them in your daily routine and they will often open up more time for you rather than take it away.

Each chapter ends with an affirmation. This is a new story that you can start telling yourself right now that will help create a new possibility in your life. We encourage you to practice these often and with enthusiasm. Affirmations have an exponentially greater impact when they are tied to positive emotions like joy, love or gratitude.

You will also find a self-observation that will help you to notice how the concept introduced in the chapter is playing out in your life right now. One of the most important things that parents can do is to see what's really going on with themselves and those around them. It's too easy just to assume that we know. Let yourself be surprised by what you might find here! Clients are often shocked and amused when they notice behaviors that have become so habitual as to be invisible to them.

Finally, we conclude each chapter with one or two exercises. These are designed to work the heart muscles and to activate the emotional brain in your journey to be a more awake parent. Just as you can't get bigger muscles simply by reading about going to the gym, it takes practice to strengthen your awake parenting capacities. But with time they will become stronger and you will have much greater control and ease as you move into more skillful, satisfying relationships with your children. You may be surprised to notice how quickly small changes can have a big impact on your life.

We recommend that you keep a journal as you engage this process. Any notebook will do just as long as it's a place to jot down your random thoughts, ideas and intuitions. The more you relate to this work, the more you will find ways to put it into action in your own life. And the more you move the thoughts you have out of your mind and onto paper, the more room you will have for new thoughts to emerge.

Maybe this all sounds a bit much for you to try on. You may feel like you don't understand your kids and that your parenting skills have been a bust. Or maybe you feel like your skills are perfect (in which case we wonder why you picked up this book). In either case, if you picked up this book, we suspect there is a longing in you for something greater than what you currently have.

If you came to our work feeling like there could be something more for you, we have a simple invitation. We are offering a new perspective on parenting that you may not have tried before and some tools that will support you in the process of waking up to all you and your family can be. We simply ask you to make a commitment to yourself to let go of your old stories temporarily and try on this perspective. Do the exercises! Your old view will be waiting for you right where you left it, ready for you to return at any point. Until then, let the journey begin!

Affirmation

Affirmations offer you the chance to support a new story and greater possibilities in your life. Throughout the book, please feel free to modify the affirmations to make them fit with your situation as well as your spiritual beliefs. As you begin this journey, we invite you to simply affirm, "I am creating loving, compassionate relationships with myself and all of my children. I am joyfully waking up more and more each day. " Try saying this ten times as you let your journey to awake parenting begin.

Self Observation

We all have different ways we relate to new ideas and information. Some resist anything new. Others will try anything but have a hard time sticking to it. Notice how you are responding to this work. Are you hopeful? Can you see ways it might open up your life? Or are you finding ways to convince yourself it will fail? How might you be approaching your whole life in the same way? Record your observations in your journal.

Practice

The more you practice, the more the ideas will become embodied and you will find it easier to engage on a daily basis with your children and loved ones. For the next few days, every morning that you wake up to your children and every evening when you return from work (or whatever times work for you) imagine that this is the first time you have ever met your family. Allow yourself to see them for the first time and experience all the possibility that comes with meeting someone new. See if you can notice things that you haven't noticed before. What surprises and delights you about these people you love?

Chapter 2: Owning Your Choices

"A man sooner or later discovers that he is the master-gardener of his soul, the director of his life."

~James Allen

Not long ago a British film called "Run, Fat Boy, Run" was released in the U.S. It was the story of a thirty something slacker named Dennis who worked as a security guard at a lingerie store. He was brokenhearted, lonely and just going through the motions. Then a strange idea came to him to run in a marathon. He wanted to prove to his family and to himself that he could accomplish something in his life.

Most runners describe something they call "hitting the wall." It's the point in a marathon when their body tells them that they simply can't continue. They are in pain, exhausted and might as well stop. This plays itself out for Dennis as he collapses onto the ground and feels he can't go on. But he changes his relationship to the experience. It's not the pain that he sees but rather he imagines the pride on his son's face as he completes the course. He gets up and hobbles across the finish line and turns a new corner in his life.

Choosing a New Relationship to Suffering

We can all relate to our experiences in any way that we choose. Spiritual teachers and psychologists throughout time have been grappling with the question of suffering. The Buddha made a particularly compelling case for transforming our relationship to suffering in what he called the Four Noble Truths. They go something like this. First, all life has suffering. Of course, we all experience pain and loss. We lose friends and lovers. People disappoint us. Sometimes we fool ourselves into believing that we are all alone, the only one that is experiencing hurt in the world, but pain is just part of the human condition.

So, if we all experience suffering why is it that some people just seem to manage better, to be happier, to not fall off balance the way others do? The Second Noble Truth is that while suffering can't be avoided, our attachment to it is what is really painful. Generally, the attachment is to what should have been.

Imagine for a moment that someone on the street randomly kicks you. It's been known to happen. You would likely experience a momentary flash of physical pain. But the story that you tell around the incident is likely to grow that pain. You might tell people how unjustly the world treats you, how this is just an example of how unsafe the world is (maybe you even buy a gun to "protect" yourself when you walk around the city), or you may tell yourself that you did something to deserve this behavior. I don't know which of these, if any, would be the "right" interpretation but considering that you will never know what was really the cause of that action (even if the person told you, you wouldn't truly understand all that had led up to that moment), you get to choose the relationship you have with the experience. You can feel the pain, accept it and move on or you can get attached to a story of what should have been and keep yourself from moving on and fully engaging your life.

This sort of attachment happens all the time. I hear it most often in the stories that people tell me of how their parents doomed them to making the choices that they make today. These stories can sound something like this. "If my mother had only loved me more, I wouldn't get angry so quickly. If my father hadn't always been away from home, I wouldn't be attracted to men who seem distant and unavailable."

You can get attached to how your children treat you as well. If your child says something hurtful to you, it can be painful. But the attachment to the fact that they shouldn't have said it, the story you tell that they don't really love you, that Sally's kid down the street never talks to her that way, all magnify the pain.

Starting to see a pattern? The common denominator in all these stories is you. Stop for a moment here and think about the places in your life that you have really experienced hurt. See if you can notice the two layers of pain. First, the actual event. Then, notice the interpretations and attachments that you make to that pain that keep it firmly embedded in your consciousness. Are these interpretations serving you? Do you find yourself making choices based on these experiences? Are these choices leading you to new possibilities or limiting you?

The Third and Fourth Noble Truths are that there is a way out of experiencing all that added pain and it's found by releasing our attachment to it. For those of you who think that's a nice idea but are convinced that you are not in control of how you react to other people or how you feel, let me suggest that the only thing that you are truly in control of is yourself. If you have ever tried to get anyone to do something that they don't want to, you know that. Deep down, we all know that the only person whose actions and thoughts that we can manage are our own. That means we are 100% responsible for our experience. We choose the story that we tell about our experiences and that story shapes how we relate to our experience creating a direct impact on all our subsequent actions.

We often fall into a habit of re-acting. We respond to the world around us unconsciously unaware of the part we actually play. So for most people it feels like those other things are running their lives. But as soon as you begin practicing new habits of awareness and responsibility the difference becomes obvious. You really are in control of your emotions. You just haven't been fully exercising it.

Let's look at an example. Two people are running around doing errands. When they come out of a particular shop, they notice that they have a parking ticket on their car for $75. Assuming that they have the same circumstances, the same amount of money, the same number of kids waiting on them, there are many different ways these two people can choose to react. The first person might get angry and stomp their feet. They decry how unfair the ticket is and how horrible life treats them. They swear and scream, jump into the car and speed away.

I don't know about you but I sure don't want to be in the car with them. Their blood pressure is racing and they're stewing in their anger. How much more likely do you think they are to have an accident? And what about the people waiting for them at home? Are they likely to get a good reception when they come in wailing about how horrible life is now that they have a parking ticket? Not only have they disrupted their day but their actions are contaminating the people around them as well. Who does any of this serve?

The second person might choose to take a very different road. They look up and realize that they have actually been parked illegally. "Thank goodness," they think, "I'm so lucky I didn't get towed. And come to think of it, how lucky I am to be among the 5% of the world's population rich enough to have a car." They put the ticket in their pocket and go on about the rest of the day. They might laugh about it later and tell their friends how fortunate they are for not getting their car towed away and how happy they are to spend time with such great friends.

We believe the choice of gratitude for what we have, even in the most difficult situations, serves us all better. The family and friends of the second person are all likely to agree. And plenty of research has shown that people with a more positive outlook on life, who are able to reframe difficult circumstances to see greater possibilities, have more friends, better relationships, better health and make more money. So who does making a different choice serve? Obviously you and everyone around you!

The big "yes but" that most of my clients want to give here is that they have no control over their emotions. They don't want to believe that they've been responsible for their previous temper tantrums, crazy behavior, and depressed jags. It's much easier to believe that they just get angry or sad or depressed and there is nothing they can do about it. And as long as they explain their experience like that, they're right. But that changes as soon as they understand that emotions don't happen to them but rather their interpretations or stories they tell about the events cause them to experience different emotions. Changing the story changes the emotion. When you dislike someone (thought: he is boring, mean, annoying, taking up too much of my time), you are happy when they leave. When you love someone (thought: she is kind, she cares for me, I like spending time with her, etc.) you are sad when she leaves. When you shift your thinking, you shift your experience of the situation.

What this means is that **you have more power than you think!** You are not a victim. You have made all kinds of choices in your life that led you to this place you are right now. And if you can own that, it means that the choices that you make in this moment can radically shift your life. You can change the direction of your sails and create something totally new or make minor adjustments and fine tune your life.

Some people have a hard time believing this. They think that life happens to them. And when we tell them how powerful they really are, they go to a place of blame and shame. In part, this is because we have been taught to hide our mistakes. We think we should be punished if we make a mistake. What a crazy thought! Not only is perfection not achievable it's also just plain boring!

Imagine if everything in life were treated the same way that learning to walk is. We could release a lot of this shame. When we are learning to walk, we fall down. We stub our toes. We might even break something. And we all know this is a part of learning. We don't stop trying to walk. We get up and keep moving.

So if your choices have brought you to a place where you feel like you have fallen down, it's okay. You are in the process of learning how to be yourself. The only shame is in staying on the ground and making up excuses as to why you are not walking. Imagine if infants said, "I'm not walking anymore because mommy yelled at me, I got scared, I peed my pants." Surely no parent would want this for their child, so why would you want it for yourself?

Let's review. We have 100% responsibility for all of our experiences and that's fine because it's okay to make mistakes (to be learning) as long as we don't deny them. These two concepts can completely shift your relationship with your children. First, anytime you have difficulties with your children when their learning process disrupts your expectations of life, you can shift over to thinking about all of the ways that you are so grateful for who they are in your life and all the joy they bring to you! You can choose to wake up to the miracle of learning that you are present to. This doesn't mean that you won't work with them to see the consequences of their actions or believe they are perfect. They don't have to be. Neither do you. But wouldn't it be more useful for you in dealing with their hiccups in learning how to be human beings to choose a more gentle relationship with those experiences?

Even more powerfully, you can help your children learn that they have control over their emotional states (occasional hormonal adjustments excluded). I often demonstrate this to clients with a simple exercise that I would invite you to use with your kids. First, ask them to think about someone in their life for one minute, a friend or family member. Think of all the negative things about that person, how they made you sad or angry. How they hurt you. At the end of the minute, notice what you would say to that person if they were standing in front of you right now. Shake this off by shaking your arms and legs. Then spend a second minute thinking nothing but loving thoughts about this person. Think about all the good things they have brought to your life, how much fun you have had with them, how excited you are to see them. At the end of the minute, reflect on how you feel about them now. What would you say to them if they were standing in front of you? In this one-minute exercise, you notice that your experience of the other person completely changes based on what you focus on, literally on the choices that you make about how to understand your experience. Your children can learn how to do this at a moment's notice and so can you!

Affirmation

Today is an exciting day! You get to take 100% control of your experience of life. Start with affirming the following statement ten times. "I joyfully accept 100% responsibility for my life today! I can choose to be as happy as I want to be! Today I will choose to relate to my life in ways that bring me joy!" Say this throughout the day.

Self-Observation

For one or two days, just notice how much of your experience is dictated by other people or circumstances. Simply laugh at yourself when you see it. There is no shame in becoming aware. Watch to see when you react as if on autopilot with other people. Write your observations in your journal and see if you notice any patterns.

Practice

This practice is a bold step into a new life. It will take practice, practice, and a little more practice. Start by picking small events to exercise choosing your reactions. You can begin with things like going to lunch or taking a walk. When something happens like your order is wrong or you have to wait a long time just take a breath and ask yourself how you would like to respond. Ask yourself what response would bring the greatest happiness to you and the other people involved in this moment. This may seem hard at first but it gets easier the more you do it until it becomes the automatic response rather than what you have been living. If you are practicing this with your children, practice with them focusing on different ways of seeing any situation and ask them which one makes them feel happier.

Chapter 3: Becoming Aware

"Within you there is a stillness and a sanctuary to which you can retreat at any time and be yourself."

~ Herman Hesse

"In stillness the world is restored."

~ Lao Tzu

Recently a client was telling me of a dilemma she was experiencing with her husband. Her three children were doing soccer and basketball and after school programs. She was feeling overwhelmed working all day, driving them around to different events, and having them come home to homework. She felt like they were all living separate lives, she confessed. She found herself fighting with her husband over having their children choose between activities rather than doing them all. She was feeling overwhelmed and missing spending time with her children that she would never be able to get back. And yet she wanted her children to have every possible opportunity in their lives. But what could she leave out without denying them vital opportunities?

The world seems to be running out of control. There are lunches to pack, dishes to wash, clothes to fold, work to be done, bills to pay and it never seems to stop. One of the defining characteristics of parents today is exhaustion. And that is getting passed onto children. They are raced from one activity to the next, bringing home hours of homework and often being forced to carry day timers to keep track of their busy lives. These high levels of stress are taking a toll on the health of children all over America showing up in higher levels of obesity, diabetes, asthma and others disorders.

Are you really here?

In a world with as many choices as ours, we simply cannot do it all. We can't see every movie, watch every TV show, play every sport, attend every concert, and still have time to be in relationships with people, to connect, open our hearts and fall in love. This desire to have it all comes from a desperate fear that we are missing something. We secretly believe the key to happiness is probably right around the corner but if we don't try everything, we just might miss it. Realizing that we are enough in this moment and that we are holding the key to happiness in our hands gives us permission to slow down and experience life rather than chasing after it like a hungry dog.

So often our heads run faster than our bodies and our hearts. We are thinking of the thousands of things that we have to do, processing the events of the day, worrying about interactions we will have later. Taking a few moments of stillness to quiet the mind and let the heart and body catch up allows for making better choices. When we only involve part of our being in making choices, we only get partially sane decisions. Acting from a place of stillness allows you to make much better choices when relating to your children.

Having your heart, head and mind in alignment is the root of stillness. For me that comes through meditation but I can also get there through breathing exercises, tai chi, going to the gym, or taking a walk. It doesn't matter how you reach stillness, just that you are able to cultivate that space in yourself where you connect to something bigger, allowing yourself to feel grounded and centered.

Often when a client comes to meet with me, I will ask them if they have arrived yet? Has all of them gotten to a point where they can have a conversation with me? This is a good question to ask yourself anytime that you are having important conversations with your children, your partner, your boss, or your friends. The more present and aligned you are, the more capable you are of really hearing what they're saying.

Take a minute and notice your level of stillness right now. First, see if you are really present as you are reading. Have you arrived? The easiest way to do this is to put your hand on your head and notice if your thoughts are bouncing around like monkeys through the treetops or if you are able to hear the ideas. Is there space for new information to land? Then put your hand on your heart and ask yourself if you are feeling emotionally open to something new. Finally, put your hand on your belly (shorthand for the body) and ask is your body is present? Are you sore, tight or tired? Are you in a position that is comfortable? Are you hungry or thirsty? Is your body in a place that you can be fully present while you are reading?

This may seem like a lot of work for a quick check in. It actually takes longer to read it than to do it. About 30 seconds is as long as most people need to bring themselves into a place of simply paying attention. It may be that you need to adjust something to be present. If you just realized you are sitting on a tack, you might want to move it. At other times, acknowledging the need is enough to create space to be more fully present. Once you know that it's there, you can address it later.

Imagine for a moment what it's like to drive a car that's out of alignment. What might you notice if the wheels and the frame don't really line up? It often feels jerky and even when we don't notice it. It can be doing damage to other systems in the car. Before we know it, the tires are worn bald, the struts are shot and we need to spend lots of time and energy to get the car repaired. Wouldn't it be easier to get the car aligned as soon as we notice something is wrong? And what if we could notice that something was out of balance very early, even before the sophisticated computers are able to?

Multitasking is often a serious sign of a lack of stillness and alignment. While it's celebrated in the workplace, it can be destructive in our personal lives. Do you enjoy talking to people who are only partially present? Have you ever had a conversation with someone who was trying to do five or six things while talking to you? When friends try to drive their cars and talk on the phone with me that's enough for me to feel like I'm only talking to half of them.

Do you ever just want to shake these distracted friends and colleagues a bit and say, "Listen, I'm trying to connect to you?" When you talk to other people from this place of busyness, do you feel like you are really connecting to them? Do you even remember what they said when you're finished talking? Is this the experience you want your children to have of you?

The most immediate change you can make in your relationship with your children is to simply stop and listen to them when they are talking to you. Listen with your whole self, your head, heart and body. Notice what you hear at each of these levels. You will be much more connected and available to your children and they'll know it. These are the moments that subtly show your children you care what they have to say and will be there when they need you.

Finding Stillness

Stillness practices don't have to take a long time. I often start with new clients by asking them to come to a place of stillness. When they are with me, we do a short meditation or breathing practice and I ask them to begin a practice of their own at home. For some this can take the form of prayer, others chant, others simply sit still and watch their breath. There are a thousand ways to be still. It doesn't matter which one you adopt.

This is also one of the places that lots of resistance arises in clients. The idea of stillness seems like a luxury for so many parents. When will there ever be time to be still? They have errands to run, children to drive to soccer games and carpool to school, lunches to pack, all in addition to what's waiting for them at work. While the notion of stillness sounds good, they simply can't figure out where to put it.

Knowing that living in chaos or crisis mode is one of the worst examples that parents can set for their children often provides an impetus to find just a few minutes a day to practice stillness. Like it or not, your children are watching everything that you do. And when you live your life on a treadmill that you can't get off of, holding on for dear life and hoping that you don't collapse, you simply don't have the resources or capacity to be present to your children.

In America, living in a world with no spaces to breathe is causing our children to be among the most stressed the world has ever known. They have higher rates of anxiety, diabetes, depression, ADD and obesity. These are all illnesses in which stress plays an enormous role. This clearly isn't serving parents or children.

The first step in getting off this crazy, 24/7 treadmill is realizing that it's crazy. Stop being in denial and come out of the closet as tired, overworked and over-stressed. Only when you've acknowledged that what you are doing in your life is not bringing you the joy and the connection that you want can you make a change.

Once you admit that some stillness might be a good idea, you will find all kinds of places to put it into your life. A stillness practice doesn't require a big commitment. I start most of my clients off with five minutes a day which they can do on the subway while they are commuting to work, in the shower or even on their bathroom break. Before they know it, they start deciding to not watch a sitcom in the evening so they can meditate a bit more (especially when they realize that the more people meditate the more weight they lose, their heart rate lowers, they get more creative and they have a higher sex drive among other benefits). Sometimes I have clients for whom five minutes a day is too much. There is no shame in this. We simply start with one minute a day and work up as they see where they can add more.

Cultivating stillness is like cultivating a vegetable garden. Most of us can't initially imagine growing acres of vegetables. And chances are we don't even need that much. But we can imagine starting with a small patch of flowers in the back yard or perhaps a couple of potted plants. The more that we care for this small plot, the more we find another plant or two would be fine as well. Be gentle with yourself as you imagine incorporating more stillness into your life. You'll be surprised what an impact even those small moments have.

We don't ask anyone to become a monk and meditate all day but rather to allow enough time in their lives for their heads, hearts and bodies to catch up with each other and to function in alignment. This allows you to be fully present to your children. When they ask you a question, it's not just your head that answers but your heart notices that there might be something deeper in the question. Maybe they need some attention or are having a problem they don't know how to express. Remember they are still in the process of learning how to communicate their needs, concerns, fears and desires.

It may take you a while to build a regular practice. It took years of starts and stops to get to the regular practice I have now. The thirty minutes a day that I meditate isn't a complicated thing. It consists of sitting still for thirty minutes at a time and simply allowing whatever is going on to happen and then bringing attention back to the breath. I am literally practicing staying balanced in a world that constantly seems to be pulling us in one direction or another. It allows me to bring my head, heart and body into alignment with each other. Even if you start with five minutes a day, there will be ripple effects throughout the whole day.

As we look for places of stillness in our lives, our families can be our greatest ally if we allow them to be. In my experience, nobody really wants mommy or daddy to be cranky. You can enlist your children in creating time for you to meditate. It might be as simple as explaining that you want to really be able to pay attention to them and be in a good mood so you will need ten minutes when you get home to fully settle in.

The most effective meditation practices that I have seen actually include the whole family in the practice! Including the family in meditation, especially when children are young, isn't as hard as you might think. You might choose a form of moving meditation such as tai chi or qi gong that allows stillness in movement. In the end, just having that time with the family is a big benefit! And on top of it, you are teaching your children how to cultivate stillness in their own lives.

Affirmation

It only takes a minute to come back to center. We can do it any time we want just by focusing on the incredible presence of our breath. In this moment, the inhale and the exhale are sustaining your life and supporting you. On your next ten breaths on the inhale say, "In any moment, I can return to my own inner stillness by simply breathing." On the exhale release anything that is holding you captive right now.

Self-Observation

The world is so busy that it's easy to miss how fast our lives are moving. Notice over the next few days when you are really being present to those around you and when you are just running on autopilot. Also notice when you are simply doing one thing like listening to people in your life with your complete attention. Make a note of the patterns that you see in your journal.

Practice

Thich Nhat Hahn, the simple Vietnamese monk who has been working tirelessly for peace in the world for years, has a simple meditation that is very practical. At least three times a day for a week, do the following exercise. Come to a place of stillness. You can be lying down, sitting or standing but just come to a stopping point and ten times breathe in deeply saying, "Breathing in I calm my body, breathing out I smile." On the exhale smile. See what a difference a breath and a smile can make!

Chapter 4: Opening Up to Gratitude

"If the only prayer you say in your whole life is Thank You, that would suffice."

~ Meister Eckhart

We exist in a seemingly infinite web of relationship that most of the time goes by completely unnoticed. We imagine that we are alone in the universe and no one is doing anything for us. We have to do it all ourselves. But even fulfilling our basic daily tasks requires teams of people who are intricately organized working behind the scenes. If you don't believe me, take a minute to realize the number of people who worked to bring a bowl of cereal to your table for breakfast. Think of the people who grew the grains, the people who turned them into cereal, the folks who made the box, and those that transported it to the store. Then there are the people who stocked the shelves and sold it to you and even the people who got you to the store by constructing your car. When I stop to think of all the work that goes into simply having a bowl of cereal I'm awestruck. And I realize how much I have to be grateful for that I don't even notice.

Before you read any further, take a moment and ask yourself a simple question. On a scale of 1 to 10, how grateful are you for your life, just exactly as it is, right now? Be honest with yourself. There are no right or wrong answers here and only you will see what you wrote down.

The Western world enjoys more wealth than the world has ever known. At every meal we eat better than most of the kings and queens throughout history. Our wardrobes are stuffed with clothes that we may rarely wear. And most of us live in homes that are loaded with more things than we actually need. We live in a time of greater freedom than most people in the world have ever known.

And yet in our world of extreme plenty, there is an almost constant background track that tells us that we should want more. Our lives are not okay. We need to keep up with the Joneses. Our minds have fallen into deep ruts of comparison and want. We look for what is wrong with us, what is missing in our lives, to figure out what we can buy or learn that will set us free.

We live our lives as if we were a giant focusing on tiny details in a microscopic world. We focus closer and closer till we can only see parts of ourselves. If we focus on our nose, we assume we are mostly a nose. We focus on our nose, make sure our skin is smooth and that we haven't accidently dipped it in the whip cream from the dessert we had at lunch (maybe that only happens to me). Before long, our world becomes all about the nose and we miss out on all the rest of who we are.

This seems like a silly example but think of how many people are focused only on how big their thighs are or the inches of their waistline. And how often they wait for whatever body part is troubling them to be "fixed" to really allow themselves to be happy. Ever had a friend tell you that she will be happy as soon as she can fit into her skinny jeans? Ever said that yourself? In the meantime, you have likely missed out on all the ways that your body is supporting you all the time and the health that you are enjoying in this moment.

Imagine that the only thing that you focused on was what was wrong with your life and what you are lacking. Maybe for life to be better you just need more money or a bigger place or a better job. All you are focusing on is what you are missing in your life and soon all you can see is what's missing. You see what's missing in yourself, your friends, your job and your family all the while missing out on the incredible beauty right in front of your face.

There's a helpful principle that I have yet to see fail with clients, friends, and family. "Energy follows attention." It means, just like when we focus on our nose, our world becomes about our nose, when we focus on what's missing in our lives, we only see what's missing. Whatever we focus on, we invite more of into our lives.

I can't make you experience gratitude for your kids when you are feeling stressed or when your boss is making you crazy. If I did that, I would be asking you to deny your experience and I would much rather you ask yourself what it's really about. Are you really mad at the kids or are you upset that you aren't getting the affection that you need? Are you really angry about the work that you have to do or are you just too tired to enjoy it? If you cover up the experience, you'll never get to the deeper truths that will lead you out of the morass. But

41

you can choose to focus on what you are grateful for in this moment.

Most us have enough to survive this moment. We have enough air to breathe. We have enough food to eat. We have enough love if we allow it. And we have enough companionship if we are open to it. But when we focus on all the things in our lives that are missing we can't see much of this. **Gratitude is a way of looking at the world that brings us wholly into the present.** It sees all that is good and allows us to breathe for a moment. When we can allow ourselves to be relaxed and in a place of ease, knowing that our needs in this moment are being taken care of, we are able to see other opportunities more clearly. It brings us back to a place of stillness.

Try this little experiment. Right now, ask yourself how you are feeling. Just check in. There's no right or wrong, just what is. Now for the next two minutes make a list of all the things that you are grateful for in your life. Think of all the people who love you, all the support that you have, all the skills that you have learned, all of the capacity that you have to move and enjoy your body, and all the people that help grow food for you to eat. What you are grateful for isn't important. Just spend two minutes writing down everything you can think of. If you have a "yes but" thought in your head just let it go for two minutes. At the end of the two minutes, look at your list, take three breaths and ask yourself how you are feeling now.

Practicing gratitude, like you just did, allows most of us to have an experience of expansion. It may feel like your heart opened up or got warm. Some people feel filled with emotion, maybe even tear up for a minute. We can choose this experience of expansiveness any time we want just by focusing on all that we have in our lives. If you think back to the principle of alignment, you might also notice that you are more present when you do this exercise. More of you is available to interact with another person. Imagine if before you went into a difficult situation you did this exercise.

I find that doing a short gratitude practice makes everything else seem smaller. Who cares if the boss didn't love your report and you have to make some changes or if your kid didn't clean up his room or if your spouse forgot to take the trash out? That's all small potatoes compared to all that you have in your life in this moment.

Go back to our initial list of what's missing. If you are focused on how you don't have enough money, you'll get what you're focused on, "not enough." A more useful choice would be to practice gratitude for all of the resources that have flowed into your life up to this point and for all of the support that you have including whatever money you are making. Then you are focusing on plenty and inviting more of it into your life. Of course, you would still take action to bring more money into your life but starting from a place of gratitude makes this a much easier process.

Anytime we are in conflict with someone, we can tend to focus on the conflict. It's likely we even imagine beforehand how mad they will be when we bring up something we assume they don't want to hear. When we focus on conflict, we usually get more conflict. When we focus on how mad they will be, we generally see mad even when that's not what they are expressing. We've already set up the lens and that's the only thing we can see through it. However, when we focus on how grateful we are for this human being in our life and how we want to create something more together, we have a completely different set of lenses to look through and usually a very different experience.

There are few places that this gratitude lens is more powerful than in our families. We can so easily focus on all the things that are wrong with our families. When we have a deep level of intimacy with people it is easy to see their faults and the ways that they have violated our expectations. We can focus just on the negative wishing that somehow our family was better. We can imagine that if our husband or wife lost weight life would be better or if our kids got better grades or if they had a better group of friends things might be different. And if we choose to see our families in this light, regardless of what we say to them, they will see themselves reflected back in that lens of lacking. When they think of themselves they will question their worth and wonder if anyone can ever truly love them, whether they will amount to anything, and whether their is anything really lovable about themselves. This is an unfortunate legacy that far too many children have received and have to overcome later in life.

However, if we use a gratitude lens to see our families we will be reflecting back how much they are loved, how worthy they are and how much potential we see in them. It is amazing how much people will rise to meet a vision of themselves that is truly great and how far they can sometimes sink to meet a vision that is small. Having gratitude for your children helps them to see where they are truly talented and assists them in striving in areas where they are not because they know that learning is possible. This seems like a far more valuable legacy to leave your children!

Affirmation

Gratitude is about bringing yourself wholly into the present and focusing, in the present moment, on all the gifts that you currently have. This affirmation is a good reminder when you are feeling stuck or as if everything is coming up manure. Say ten times, "I am seeing all the gifts that I have been given in this moment. I am joyfully receiving all the universe has to offer!"

Self-Observation

We often only notice the things that bug us, the fly in our ointment, so to speak. But there is much more to notice. For the next several days, let yourself experience how amazing your children are as well as yourself. How many ways are you surprised and enlivened by what they do? What gifts have gone unnoticed or forgotten? What ways do they practice care or compassion for you or other family members? Write your observations in your journal.

Practice

People don't write letters very often. This week write one letter everyday. You can write them to each of your children, to your partner, to your parents, to yourself expressing all that you are grateful for that they have brought to your life. You can write these letters to people who have passed on or to people that you are not quite ready to send them to. If you choose not to send them, remind yourself of all that you felt when you wrote your letter next time you talk with them.

Chapter 5: Creating Space for Abundance

"There is a treasury of joy within you, why do you keep knocking door to door?"

~ *Sufi saying*

How much oxygen can you hold in your lungs? If you were simply to inhale without ever exhaling, it would be a very limited amount and your life would be greatly shortened. But if you allow yourself to release the oxygen you are currently holding you are able to fill up again and again. This is the main truth of abundance. **Abundance begins with release.** No matter how much we have, we will only receive more when we are willing to share what we have already received. This is true of all forms of energy in the universe.

The practice of gratitude is seeing what only comes when we allow ourselves to receive and to be abundant. In other words, gratitude is about paying attention, seeing what is and choosing to focus on where life is showing up. Abundance is learning to allow yourself to live in our amazing universe as an owner rather than as a squatter.

Many parents are working out of a scarcity parenting model. It's usually inherited from parents who didn't really see us well enough to meet our most fundamental needs. They may have been trying very hard to love us but somehow it didn't translate in the ways we needed them to.

There are three main characteristics that show up in this model. In our culture scarcity is the dominant perspective. This makes it difficult for parents not to incorporate at least some of this into their parenting practices.

First, scarcity-based parents believe there is a limited supply of energy to fill the needs of themselves and their children. There is only so much love, appreciation, kindness or compassion that is available in them to give to themselves and their children. Because they often misunderstand their children's primary needs as physical (such as new toys, clothes, money), they can feel inadequate and often ashamed of their inability to provide all that is needed. This can lead to subtle breaks in relationship with children as parents move to protect themselves from the hurt of failing their children. It can also lead to anger when children don't respond to the things that their parents give them in the way they expect.

Second, because there is a limited supply of energy to meet the needs of all, they can often feel in competition with their children. This can be hard to admit because parents can feel like they must sacrifice their own happiness to meet the needs of the children or vice versa. How could it be otherwise? If there are only five apples on the table and six mouths to feed, someone is not going to get an apple. This can lead to parents that operate in a sacrificial or martyrdom role. They give to their children and weaken themselves. But in a world that requires parents to function as strong role models, this doesn't work so well.

Third, they misunderstand the source of energy, life, love, and abundance. They see these things as internally generated rather than readily available for anyone who is open to receiving them. This leads to exhaustion and the belief that the parent is not enough. In addition, it robs children of learning how to draw from much larger sources to support their own needs.

In the end, this scarcity model of parenting makes people feel small and competitive. "Every person for themselves" and "Looking out for Number 1," become the only real options. Parents compete for opportunities for their children and believe that in this limited pool of resources they can't share with other parents or else their children will be deprived. Unfortunately, teaching our children scarcity only leads to lonely, disconnected adults. I haven't met any parents who really want that for their children.

The alternative to living in scarcity is a life lived in abundance. Try this on for a minute. Imagine that you lived in an enormous mansion complete with a conservatory for playing music, libraries for reading, gyms for exercising, parties being thrown where you are the guest of honor, an indoor swimming pool, flowers and fruit trees, and in the midst of all that, you choose to live in the broom closet behind the back stairs. This is a life lived in scarcity. It is far too easy to live in an abundant universe with our eyes closed missing out on

47

everything that's available if we could only see.

When we allow ourselves to receive and pay attention to what we are receiving, we realize that all of us are living in such a great mansion. This is the life of abundance. But most of us choose to live in fear that what we have now will go away or not be enough in the future. This scarcity mentality is the root of hoarding that so many in the West currently engage in. We fill our refrigerators so full that food expires and fill our closets so full we have wardrobes greater than most of history's kings and queens. And holding onto what we have, we are often not willing to support others in need with our time, money and other resources. This is not to say that there are not economic hardships or that times aren't often stressful. But at its core, **abundance is about letting the now be enough.** We can't really live in anything beyond this moment so we allow it to hold and sustain us.

Scarcity is rarely experienced in the present to the extremes that it shows up in our minds. At some point during my work with many of my clients, we work on something psychologists call "anticipatory anxiety." This means that they get focused on what might happen. With limited information they begin to imagine all of the worst possible scenarios. Maybe the meeting that their boss has set up with them is to lay them off. Maybe their girlfriend will hate them if they ask for what they need. Maybe no one really likes them and if they throw a party no one will come and they will know it's true once and for all. I bet you have a list of your own. And generally, none of this serves you very well.

When we choose to live in fear of what might happen, we are living in the smallest part of ourselves. Not only does this miss out on all that really exists around us, we tend to isolate and disconnect from universal abundance. Isolation rarely helps us decrease our anxiety any more than imagining negative possibilities. For most people imagining the worst possible scenario can be completely immobilizing making them much less capable in the event that an actual crisis does occur. Take a moment to notice where this is true for you. Where do you attach to the possibility of a negative outcome even before it has the chance to happen? Do you feel like this is serving you?

In America we are living through a particularly stark period of anticipatory anxiety. Many people have decided that the next great depression is right around the corner and there is little that will dissuade them from that view. They horde their resources and wall themselves off from the world. Others are living in fear of global warming and ecological disaster and yet doing little to nothing to change that outcome. Anticipatory anxiety calls us back into the smallest parts of ourselves. But, as Deepak Chopra noted in a recent article for the *San Francisco Chronicle*, it is exactly in times of crisis that we are called upon to expand rather than to contract. It is in times of need that we are called to share all the resources that we do have so that everyone can prosper.

Our world is not just our dollars. It is also our communities, our connections, the love we have, the skills we bring, the resources that we can share and the care that we can offer one another. When we each give what we have, there is always enough for everyone. When we each realize the amazing levels of abundance we experience in the richest country on the planet, then we can release our small selves that are steeped in scarcity.

Practicing abundance in our families requires that we turn the scarcity model upside down. When you trust the following understandings of abundance, you can open up to your children in a way you never dreamed possible.

First, **we are not the source** of life energy, love, compassion, hope or any of the things that we want to pass onto our children. We aren't even the source of the things that we want to give them. Humans are still hunters and gatherers. We share the energy of the land to make our lives possible. While the energy of the land is finite, the energy required to meet our emotional needs is infinite. It grows and expands each time we share it with others. It is love, compassion, hope and imagination that really meet our needs.

Second, **our universe is abundant enough for us all**. There is enough food to feed everyone, there is enough housing to house everyone and there are enough resources to go around. We may have to think creatively or to call others to accountability but there are physically enough resources. And once our basic survival needs are met, we know that there is enough emotional energy to go around. Simply by sharing it, we create more. This is what we are really longing for anyway.

Third, since there is enough, **we can afford to be generous**. You don't have to take on the role of victim or sacrificial lamb to meet the needs of your kids nor do you have to withhold so that you can take care of yourself. There may be times when physical resources are not available to us and we have to make hard decisions. It may not be possible to do everything that we like to do or have all of the things we would like. But we will never run short on emotional energy to fuel us as long as we are open to receiving it.

When parents adopt an abundance model of parenting they foster children who are loving, open and generous. They offer their hearts and their resources generously. In fact, if you watch very young children you know this is their natural state. There exists in us a basic desire to share and take care of the needs of others that is innate. The most powerful statement of Jesus is simply, "Ask and it will be given." If we are willing to risk trusting that we just might live in a universe that is on the side of life, love and compassion, we can risk asking for what we really need. We can become vulnerable to receiving abundance in our lives. And we can teach the same level of openness and peace to our children.

Affirmation

Abundance is about allowing ourselves to receive all the gifts that the universe is offering us in this very moment. That requires us to believe we deserve them. Say ten times, "I am abundance. I deserve all of the gifts that the universe is offering me right now."

Self-Observation

Notice for the next few days how often you stop yourself from receiving something. What stops you? In what ways are you hoarding your time, love, money, energy, and compassion from yourself and from other people? Write your observations in your journal.

Practice

When you were in school, if you went on a field trip, you had to have a permission slip from your parents. Now, you are the authority in your life and you can give yourself permission to do anything you choose. Copy the following permission slip, sign it and carry it with you as a daily reminder.

Permission Slip

I, _____, joyfully give myself permission to receive all of the gifts that the universe is offering me in this moment. I am worthy of receiving freely. I will allow myself to share these gifts openly knowing that sharing simply invites more abundance into my life.

_____

(Your signature here)

Chapter 6: Releasing Others from Your Expectations

"Expect nothing, live frugally on surprise."

~ Alice Walker

I am not the most computer savvy person in the world. Don't get me wrong, I like surfing the net as much as the next person and I can even type without looking at the keys, at least not too much. But I do find the way much of my software works somewhat mystifying.

As I was sitting at my desk working on this chapter, I noticed that my computer was doing strange things. All of the sudden, a bar disappeared that I was used to seeing on the right hand side of the screen and along with it the page numbers that are usually located on the bottom of the page. I wasn't sure what had happened but I started to get frustrated. The computer is supposed to make my life easier not do strange things. And what would happen if the whole document simply disappeared? Would I lose all the work I'd been doing?

Before long I was grumbling away at the computer. Why didn't this thing just work the way it was supposed to? Why didn't those insane program monkeys at Microsoft make software that was reliable? And on and on my mind went with this until somewhere a little laughter started to break through. Even as I was writing a chapter on letting go of expectations and letting life show up as it is, I was getting hung up on my own expectations. I decided instead just to save, take a few minute break and restart. When I came back to my work, everything seemed to be in order. Even if it hadn't been, I was in a much more resourceful state to deal with whatever problems the computer might have planned for me. Thank goodness this all happened when I was writing this chapter.

Life has a funny way of showing up differently than we plan. If you've ever thrown a party, you know that you never really know how it's going to go until it happens. There is a delicate balance of planning a good party, having enough food, inviting the right people and allowing it to happen. If you try to control the flow of a party by planning every moment there is simply no room for spontaneity and surprise to show up. The control can choke the life out of a group of people who would otherwise find their own relationships and connections.

When we levy this kind of control upon our friends and loved ones through our expectations, we can choke the life out of these relationships as well. Abundance in our relationships begins with releasing people and situations from our expectations and allowing them to show up as themselves.

This isn't something that we practice very often. From our very earliest days, we start setting up roles that other people play. Our teachers control the classroom and rarely share their emotions or even their own opinions. "Just the facts." Our parents provide for our needs. The trash collectors pick up the trash. The grocery clerk sells us our groceries. Pretty soon we begin to act as if everyone is a product of their function. We stop seeing the grocery clerk as a human being, forget to say hi and connect. We begin to see people in rigid roles. Even when they do show up differently, it's hard for us to break out of the old story we've been telling about them. And when they do something unexpected, we aren't sure how to react. How would you feel if the next time you bought gas, the cashier asked to give you a hug or handed you a flower?

Test this out for yourself. Do you expect that your boss will act substantially differently tomorrow than she did yesterday? Do you expect that your partner will act differently tomorrow than today? For most of us, we expect that short of a life-changing event people show up pretty much the same from day to day. So we can load our "boss program" or our "partner program" or even our "children program" and go on autopilot. We can treat them the same today as we did yesterday.

Keep in mind this program is often not very pleasant. Carrie was a client who was really frustrated with her boss. Since the day her new boss walked in the door, he had done nothing but dis-empower and micromanage her. And she was mad as hell and ready to go find another job.

While I agreed that this clearly wasn't a good experience, I asked Carrie if she would like to stay in this position if she could find a way to enter into a new kind of relationship with her boss that would give her more freedom. The thought hadn't crossed her mind but she was willing to give it a try. I asked her to begin with a simple shift. She had been looking for all the ways that her boss was acting like a complete ogre and that seemed to be all she could see. So I asked her to find one thing a day that she could actively appreciate about her new boss. By "actively appreciate," I mean tell him via email or even a simple thank you that he was appreciated. The only criteria was that it had to be true.

It didn't take long for her to start to have a new perspective on her boss. It wasn't that she thought her boss was always right or that she loved the way he behaved. However, allowing her boss to defy her expectations gave her a point of entry into his experience. He was nervous about taking on a big new responsibility with people he didn't know. This opening allowed her to try on new behaviors with her boss that substantially shifted her relationship with him. She is now enjoying her job again and has managed to build a significant relationship with her boss so that she could stay in the job that she loved.

It may have been that Carrie couldn't find the connection that she desired and discovered that it was time to move onto another job. That would have been fine too. Releasing people from your expectations isn't about doing nothing but rather it's about creating shifts in yourself that allow for more flexibility. No matter what she discovered, she would have been able to see more clearly beyond her perceptions and act accordingly.

We know that we have changed a lot in our lives. We can probably point to radically different ideas that we have now than we did when we were ten or twenty-five or forty. Most of have experienced changes in relationships, friends that have come and gone, people that have passed on, and even marriages that have begun and ended. And all of us know that our bodies have changed as we have aged. We've gotten taller or wider or stronger or grayer. Maybe the status of our health has changed over time. And yet, we still like to believe that people are staying pretty much the same.

Believing that people don't change often, in spite of the overwhelming evidence to the contrary, makes organizing our world easier. How could we believe that things aren't changing all the time?

The human body alone is always changing. Not one cell in your entire body will be the same seven years from now as it is today. One idea that influences you today can change your whole way of being in a year. The great gift of being human is that we are able to consciously reflect on our ideas, our hopes, and our dreams and find a new direction at any moment.

But in the midst of immense change, our expectations function as a kind of container to make life seem more reliable and safe. These aren't bad things to want. Everyone wants this at some level, otherwise we would run out into traffic in the highway just for the pure thrill of the adrenaline rush. But in our pursuit of stability, we often undermine our deepest longing by not seeing the other person fully. As we hold them hostage to our expectations, they are suffocated. As long as they stay the same, we are not forced to rewrite our programs. Life can keep moving forward in a comfortable progression. But this can be very destructive to the actual people in our lives. Its very easy for our expectations to become like a straightjacket for those that we most love. And soon, they begin to resent us for keeping them locked in a role that they no longer want to play.

The most common expectation among families is that our partners will meet our needs. We make them "special" for us and expect that they will make us feel special too. When they don't, our capacity for intimacy and love shrink. We start to resent them and from there it doesn't take long before they start to wonder what's wrong with us. Ever wonder why so many marriages end up in divorce? It seems that at least one factor is this pattern of "special" relationship that our culture reinforces at every turn.

You might take a moment now and just ask yourself which of your needs you have made your partner's responsibility. Do you need her to make sure you feel appreciated? Do you need him to make you feel secure? No matter what our expectation of the other, when there is no room for flexibility, we can quickly move into the danger zone. How do you feel when your partner doesn't fulfill your expectations? How does it affect your relationship?

I recently heard a funny story of a wife who wanted to go out to dinner. Even before her husband got home she decided that he would be too tired to go. When her husband opened the front door,she looked at him and simply grunted, "Hmmph." The husband knew that wasn't a good sound but was totally dumbfounded.

"What?" he said.

"You're too tired to go out to dinner."

"I am?" he asked, starting to believe it.

"Just go sit on the couch and watch TV."

"Okay," replied the husband, still somewhat confused.

We can laugh at these stories because we know that we have all done things just like this. At times, we have all let our expectations define other people in our lives. What have you decided about your partner before you even ask? Is there any possibility that, if you chose to ask, you would get an answer that surprises you?

Parents can often act (even if it's subconscious) in a way that puts their children into a specific role in the family. Maybe they are the problem child that can't seem to get it right, or they are the smart one that is expected to be perfect, or the responsible one that should be capable of making wise choices. The "smart child" can come to feel like they can't ask for help because they are supposed to know the answers. The "problem-child" can come to believe they can't find something to excel at since it would disrupt the family system.

Much of Dan's work revolves around working with families where a child has taken on the mantle of addict. Before you know it, the whole family is focused on how this child is disruptive. What can be done about this problem? And they fail to notice how their own expectations and roles have played into the choices that their child has made. While this is an extreme case, trying to fit children into rigid expectations that don't make sense for them often leads them to seek whatever form of escape that is the most readily available to them.

Take a moment now and see if you can identify what role or expectations you put on your children, your partner, and yourself. What roles do you feel are placed on you? Ask yourself where these notions come from. And whether they are serving you?

The expectations we place on others largely come from trying to externally meet our needs that we could be meeting internally. There is a funny story taught by many Buddhist teachers in which a man taking an evening stroll comes across another man on his hands and knees frantically searching under a lamp post. They begin to talk and the first man finds out that the second has lost his keys. He gets on the ground and begins to help him. Finally the second man asks him if he is sure he lost his keys here. The first man replies, "No. I lost them at home but I can see better here."

We are often looking for pieces of ourselves that we think other people have. Choosing to be our own source of love, compassion, intimacy, and kindness allows others to show up for us in a way that is more loving and compassionate. When we stop looking for a person to act in a particular way, we begin to see all the other ways that they are expressing their love, compassion, kindness and intimacy with us.

One of the most powerful ways that we can love our families is to release them from our expectations. It's only natural that we should have hopes and dreams for our family members. We can often see great potential in them that they are unable to see in themselves praising them for their accomplishments and their efforts. Reflecting back their greatness can go far in helping children to gain self-worth but making them responsible for meeting our expectations of who they will be is a burden that is too difficult to bear for any child.

If you are able to allow your children to show up exactly as they are, you will actually be able to see how they are changing right before your eyes. It will be just like it was when you watched them learn to walk and talk. Perhaps they were clumsy at first but learning is always clumsy, at least a little bit. Besides, there's nothing fun about perfection!

The same goes for you. The more you are able to show up fully in the moment free of expectations, the more flexibility you will have to act freely and compassionately. You will be open to following your heart. So give yourself a break and realize that the person you are is worth letting other people get to know.

Affirmation

Expectations are largely stories that we tell ourselves about how other people fit into our lives. Imagine co-authoring the story so that the people in your life can tell their own part. Say the following affirmation ten times and practice throughout the rest of the day. "I am releasing my expectations of everyone I meet. I am joyfully allowing them to show up exactly as they are!"

Self-Observation

Spend a few days starting to notice where you have placed expectations on others in your life. What do you expect from your partner, your children, your boss and your own parents? Record your observations in your journal.

Practice

When people fail to meet our expectations, we can feel angry or hurt. We can often make their actions about us. They did this TO ME. For this week, pick one or two people in your life that you have expectations of. Enter all your interactions with them realizing that they are simply trying to meet their needs the best they can and just like you they are not as skillful as they might like to be. Make a commitment to allow them to show up just as they are. Realize that you don't need them to be any different than they are in just that moment. And in that interaction find some small way to express your gratitude for them in your life just as they are. It can be a hug, telling them you are glad to see them, giving them a flower or any other way that you feel works. Notice what changes occur in this relationship as you engage the practice.

Chapter 7: Loving Deeply

"Years ago I recognized my kinship with all living things, and I made up my mind that I was not one bit better than the meanest on the earth. I said then and I say now, that while there is a lower class, I am in it; while there is a criminal element, I am of it; while there is a soul in prison, I am not free."

~ Eugene Debbs

Our world can feel very isolating. There are days when we feel all alone, as if no one really understands us and probably never will. Those days are exhausting. They can make most of us want to crawl back in bed and hide under the covers.   Parents, especially single parents, can feel this sense of isolation particularly intensely.

Philosophers and spiritual teachers have often described the basic struggle of humanity as our attempt to return to a state of oneness.   This sense of deep separation is found in many spiritual texts like the Judeo-Christian story of the Garden of Eden where Adam and Eve are cast out of the garden and separated from God.   It seems that we have been trying to get back to that state of oneness or connection in one way or another since the beginning of time.

At the root of compassion lies an understanding of the deeply interconnected nature of the universe. It understands that what we do to one person affects all people.   Matthew and Terces Englehart, founders of Café Gratitude, like to talk about humans as cells in the body of humanity.   It is impossible for the actions of one set of cells to avoid triggering a chain reaction of events that affect the whole rest of the body.

When our primary experience of the universe is one of separation, it's hard not to live "looking out for number one."   Albert Einstein, who himself had something of a mystic edge, understood that life is deeply interconnected.   We can even go so far to say that relationship is the foundational organizational principle of the universe. Einstein wrote, "A human being is a part of the whole, called by the universe. A part limited in time and space. He experiences himself, his thoughts and feelings, as something separate from the rest, a kind of optical delusion of his consciousness. This delusion is a kind of prison for us, restricting us to our personal desires and to affection for a few persons nearest to us. Our task must be to free ourselves from this prison by widening our circle of compassion to embrace all living creatures."

Take a minute and ask yourself, on a scale of 1 to 10, how connected do you really feel to your family, your friends, the world around you and to nature? You probably feel more connected in some areas than others, as well as more connected to some people than others. If you describe yourself as lonely, disconnected or depressed, chances are you are not feeling the deep interrelatedness that holds us all together in a giant web of life.

In the context of the family, this means that all our thoughts, words and actions affect those around us. Henry Grayson, author of <u>Mindful Loving</u>, tells of an experiment he once performed on his wife. (He does not recommend others try this at home.) He spent every other day for two weeks thinking, throughout the day, either of his wife in a completely loving way, focusing on all the wonderful things that she brought to his life or in a terrible way, thinking of all her faults and the things that were wrong with her. He reports that on the days that he was feeling loving towards her, when he arrived home, she was most often happy to see him and they spent time connecting with each other. On the days where he thought critical and judgmental thoughts, he often found his wife just as critical back to him, ready to fight or absent altogether. Some psychologists refer to what Grayson was doing as "priming the pump." When we think compassionate thoughts about someone, or positive thoughts about an activity, we are more likely to see the positive. When we think negative thoughts, the reverse is also true.

This is a small example of the way that compassion, being able to hold another in our heart and relate to them, can affect relationships. Jesus expresses this deep sense of interconnection in his command to love everyone who crosses your path and give freely even to those most disconnected from you. He says, "As you do to the least of these, you have also done to me."

Buddhists have a meditation practice where they hold people in compassion, as a mother would hold her child, as a way of bringing love and kindness to that person. They do this not only to people that are loving them back or they think are worth loving, they do this also for the people in the world that have done great harm, have caused intense suffering and sometimes are called monsters.

At the deepest levels, compassion is about being able to see that there is no us and them. We all hold the seeds of great love as well as the seeds of destruction. When we hide from our own shadow side, we have to make other people the enemy or other. They provide somewhere to project all the grossness that we don't want to see is also in ourselves.

The practice of compassion begins with seeing ourselves in both our shadow and our light, and holding ourselves gently in whichever form we show up. When we lose our temper and lash out at people, when we cause great harm, when we feel completely unlovable, we hold ourselves in compassion. When we act from the places of our deepest wisdom, when we are at our most skillful, when we bear witness to all that humanity is capable of, we hold ourselves in compassion.

We have all probably heard flight attendants many times say if the cabin pressure should drop and the oxygen masks appear, first put them on yourself and then help those around you. The same is true for compassion. When we give ourselves the gift of compassion, we are releasing ourselves from the need to be perfect, to be better than others, understanding that we are both as good and as evil as every person that we meet. We are all trying the best we can, in our own sometimes bumbling ways, to make our way on this journey called life.

The arch enemy of compassion is judgment. When we deem other people "good" or "bad," we are assigning value to their worth as a human being. Ever hear someone say, "He's just no good." Anytime that we judge a person rather than their actions we are disconnecting from them. When we tell a child that they are bad, this registers deeply in their psyches, especially if they hear it over and over again. You might think that telling them they are "good" would be the answer but this is still an external judgment that you pass upon them. The result in either case is a questioning of worth when, in reality, our basic human value cannot be judged. We are all children of God, Allah, the sacred, the divine or however you understand that which is larger than you and connects us all.

This does not mean that we cannot judge the actions of others. But even saying that an action is bad or good is generally too broad a statement to be useful. What does that mean? Is the person bad because their action was? Are they good if their actions are? And how tied are our expectations to what we understand as good or bad?

There is an old story from the East about a father. The story begins when one of his best horses runs away. The whole village wants to commiserate with how bad this situation is.

The man simply says, "We'll see."

A few days later the runaway horse returns with a whole pack of wild horses. And the village wants to rejoice with him in his good fortune. Again, the man simply says, "We'll see."

A few days later, the man's son is training one of the horses when he is thrown. He crashes to the ground and breaks his leg. And all of the village people want to decry his fate. And once again, the man simply says, "We'll see."

A month passes and the army comes through conscripting all of the young men of the village off to war. Only his son, with his leg in a cast, is not taken off to fight in the war.

It is often difficult even to know how to judge an action. This is particularly true when we don't know what its outcome will be. How many times have you broken up with the "love of your life" feeling that you simply couldn't go on only to find someone better? Or perhaps you have lost a job that you loved only to find something much more fulfilling later. I know this has been true for me.

Buddhists are fond of talking about actions as skillful or unskillful. Understanding that all of us are trying to meet our needs in the ways that we know how, we can judge whether an action brings about the particular condition that it intended. "Good" actions generally meet the needs of the person while creating the conditions of the person they want. While "bad" actions that people do might meet their immediate needs but fail to produce the conditions they desire. These actions are an indication that more learning is required rather than they are bad people.

Let's take a very basic example. When I was very young, when a boy wanted to get the attention of a girl, he would often pull her hair or tell her that she had cooties. Clearly, this did not meet his goal of getting closer but it did manage to engage her in some form of connection. It took more skills in relating and even learning how to flirt until he was really able to figure out how to deeply connect.

When we hold ourselves in compassion, honestly seeing the ways that our actions are unskillful, we are able to make another choice. But often, we aren't able to see where we can change our level of skillfulness. It can require the aid of a friend or even a skilled coach to help us acquire the skills that we need to engage the world in a more useful fashion.

Take a minute now and notice if there are places in your life that you are not accomplishing what you would like. Are your relationships with your family members going the way you would like? Are you accomplishing all that you would like to in your work? Do you have the kind of spiritual or personal growth practice that you might like? If not, ask yourself if there are any places that you can see where you might need to improve your skills to get what you want? You can check your observations out with a trusted friend or colleague.

Parents are often unskillful in meeting their own needs and they can easily pass these patterns on to their children. In fact, they are often repeating the unskillful habits of one or both of their parents. For example, if you yell at your children when you want them to quiet down, is it any surprise that they yell or throw a temper tantrum when their needs are not being met? Asking yourself what need that your child is unskillfully trying to achieve in their current actions gives you an entry point into their world that is incredibly powerful. You then have the space to ask them if, indeed, they are trying to meet that need and teach them how they might get what they are after. Compassion, like abundance, creates opportunities for expansion and learning, where judgment only breeds unmet needs, anger and shame. Wouldn't you rather teach your children skillful ways of being in the world?

Affirmation

Compassion opens up the heart to yourself and to your children. It creates a sense of possibility and expansiveness. Say the following affirmation ten times now and throughout the day. "I am holding myself in loving compassion. I am worthy. When I am unskillful, I choose to learn new skills and open to life!"

Self-Observation

Take a few days to notice where you are judging other people in your life. What are the judgments you are putting on them? Are they good? Bad? In what ways are these judgments things that you also really believe about yourself? Write down your observations in your journal.

Practice

We can choose to open our heart to anyone we want. Using this simple guided meditation, you can radically alter your experience of anyone. For one week do the following meditation directed at a person that you are holding lots of judgments against. See how your relationship changes!

First, call to mind someone that you deeply love. See their face in your mind, feel the love that you know they feel for you. Rest in that love and compassion for a few moments. Then direct all the compassion that you feel for them into your own heart knowing that you are worthy of great love and compassion. Sit in that compassion for a few minutes feeling your heart opening up all the time. Finally, move that compassion to someone you are having difficulty with. Know that they too are worthy of great love. They are simply trying the best they know how to meet their own needs. Rest in that knowledge.

Chapter 8: Building on Practice

"An ounce of practice is worth more than tons of preaching."

~ Ghandi

"Live with intention. Walk to the edge. Listen hard. Practice wellness. Play with abandon. Laugh. Choose with no regret. Appreciate your friends. Continue to learn. Do what you love. Live as if this is all there is."

~ Mary Anne Radmacher

Whether you know it or not, your children are paying attention to you all the time. They might not seem to hear what you say or do what you tell them, but they are watching your actions. That means that you teach your children far more from what you do than from what you say. In fact, studies have repeatedly proven that about 80% of our communication comes from our actions. The most profound changes in your family can only come from shifting your behavior.

Seeing a broken or unskillful pattern of behavior is not enough to create lasting, sustainable change. Only practice creates change that's embodied. Wouldn't it be great if you started practicing greater compassion and gratitude in your life and your children started following your example? What an amazing gift to pass on to them!

I have to admit that one of my guilty pleasures is watching TV shows that help families become healthier. I know it's reality TV but at least it has a good intention, right? I'm often amazed to watch parents show up with obese children and act as if their children are not following their example. For the most part, the size and shape of the child mirrors that of the parent. When the parents shift their values and start telling a new story about health this is a strong shift towards new behaviors. But for change to really anchor itself into a family, the parents have to change their way of eating and exercising. When their kids see them eating vegetables, passing on dessert or going for a walk after dinner, only then does lasting shift occur.

Most of us can see at least some of our own patterns of unskillful behavior when we choose to. We are armed with a psychological vocabulary and toolkit that was unheard of 100 years ago. And many people have incredibly strong inner critics that seem to always be pointing out what they are doing wrong. But translating those insights into actual behavior shifts is tricky. Of course, it can be hard to figure out exactly what we should do to change things. But even when we know, it can be hard to motivate ourselves to change. We will be the first to tell you that just like you can't get bigger muscles simply laying on the couch, creating better relationships with your family is going to take some work. Maybe even a little self-discipline.

The good news is that every single person that I have ever met has more practice at being disciplined than they realize. Even though lots of people tell me stories about themselves where they define themselves as lazy, incapable or just plain no good, we almost always have greater capacity than we think. In fact, when there is something that we really want, we are virtually unstoppable.

Maybe you don't believe me. Here's a little list that I would like you to consider. Chances are you have mustered the energy, excitement and courage to practice until you were able to do these things with at least some degree of skill.

- Crawling, standing up and walking

- Reading - pretty complicated feat if you ask us

- Riding a bike, swimming, skipping, jump roping

- Operating a cell phone, a VCR, a computer, maybe even a TIVO (I'm still working on that one)

- Kissing, holding hands, having sex (lots of you reading this have children, don't you?)

Take a moment to add to this list. Add all of the things that you have mastered in your life. Maybe it's speaking a foreign language or playing a sport or a musical instrument. Maybe its learning how to bake a cake or cook a pot roast. These are all examples of your capacity, through disciplined effort, to create a new skill in your life. In all of these cases, the reward was greater than the work you had to do to reach it. Your passion and vision carried you forward.

Now do a quick mental inventory. Use the last week (or at least the last typical week you had). List all of the time that you spent working on being a more skillful parent. Include time spent practicing something, reading a book, strategizing with a friend or loved one. Be generous with yourself on this list. You can include anything you want as long as it's not your usual parenting duties that have become pretty automatic. Now, take a second quick inventory of all of the time that you spent watching TV, reading books or magazines, or doing whatever you do to entertain yourself. Compare these two figures. For most of the people we work with, the second figure is far greater than the first. What would happen if you shifted some of your entertainment time to skill building time? How might your family benefit?

Learning a new habit or way of being can be hard. Particularly in the beginning, when you might not see the immediate benefit, it can be challenging to keep up the work. For anyone who has ever worked out, you know that it takes months to see the actual results of going to the gym but subtle changes are going on all the time. The same is true in learning a new skill.

Most people approach a behavior change with all the will power they can muster. They marshal their resources and prepare to charge. How many times have you started a new diet or exercise program full speed ahead only to peter out on your commitment by the second or third day? Most of us have had this happen.

Using willpower as the primary engine to power change is particularly exhausting. Most of the people I work with are already feeling pretty overwhelmed. People can often feel exhausted when they come to us and asking them to do one more thing can feel completely impossible.

An easier way to create change is to enlist the power of the unconscious mind to hold us up as we move forward. I use hypnosis and story to do this with most of my clients. Imprinting positive images in the self conscious mind of you achieving the results you want and feeling good about them can go a long way in quieting those pesky little voices that suggest you can't do it anyway, so why even try. Simply imagining what you want to have in your life very concretely with great feeling is an easy way of doing this for yourself which we will cover in a later chapter.

For now, simply know that you can start to shift your stories and the new stories you tell will help you as you engage new practices. Let me give you an example. I like working with people who have been trying to lose weight but never seem to move forward. In part, this is because they have been working very forcefully to create change and when they get exhausted and quit they feel bad about themselves. When I work with them to discover new stories, they gain greater self esteem and wake up to themselves.

Imagine the story you were telling yourself was that you were a bad person because you had extra weight around your waist or your thighs. That seems like a pretty shallow criteria to judge your worth as a human but our culture supports that message. The story that you would have told is essentially a tale of battle. You are advancing your energy to stomp out the evil fat that is trying to encroach upon your sense of self worth. In this story, much of the body becomes the enemy.

In contrast, when I work with weight loss clients, we find a new story that allows them to see their whole body wanting to support them in feeling good. And I help them to imagine themselves healthy, strong and full of energy. Once they know that's possible in the future, they begin to tell themselves a story that they are a healthy, capable person making choices that support their well-being. Can you see how different these two experiences are? Once the new story is in place, their behaviors shift to align with their new story.

I wonder what story you are telling about your parenting practices and change? Are you telling yourself that changing your behaviors will be hard? No fun? Painful? Or are you telling yourself that you are an amazingly capable person who has achieved so much in your life and that any changes you choose to make will be simple and worthwhile. You might even imagine yourself parenting in the way that you want with your children, having the relationship that you would like and enjoying how good it feels to connect in this new way.

The stories that we tell are a primary support for practicing new behaviors. There are two others that I find very useful in helping clients shift long held patterns of behavior. One is purpose, which we talk about in depth in the next chapter. The other is commitment.

When we get married, we make a commitment to stay with each other and try to work things out even if they aren't always great. This stated commitment keeps us going longer than we might if we didn't really care and could just walk away from each other. Wedding vows are a commitment that many of us make in front of our friends and family. There is often a point in religious services where the witnesses of the union are asked if they too will support this couple and their relationship. We invite the assistance of our friends and family in this endeavor because we know that support from our community strengthens our ability to meet our commitments.

When we want to make a change in our lives, one of the strongest supports we can have is a friend or family member who believes we are capable of making that change. They get to be our external imagination that holds the picture of us achieving exactly what we want to even when we are feeling tired or frustrated and we just want to give up.

Take a moment now and think of who can support you in your commitment to becoming more awake in your parenting. Could you share these ideas with your partner, another single parent, a church group or a friend? Consider asking one of these people, if not more, to support your efforts.

Our commitments, both big and small, are essentially what define us. We declare to the universe, and more important, ourselves, that we choose to move forward with our lives, do something new and change an old pattern of behavior. When we keep our commitments with ourselves, we build a pattern of shift that allows new patterns to be created in the future. Whether they are spoken or unspoken, meeting or breaking our commitments teaches us who we are.

You can choose today to be a commitment to awake parenting. You can be a commitment to loving and compassionate being with your children (and your wider community if you so choose). Making choices like this create a momentum in you that allows you to keep going even when the going gets tough. Isn't that the example you want to provide your kids?

When our commitment to change is married to a deep passion, a desire so strong that we can taste it, there is little that can stop us from achieving what we are after. Look back to your list of all the things that you have been able to learn in your life when they were important to you. How much more important are your children and your own well-being in the world? Knowing that you are firmly committed to your family, the practice is much easier to engage and the more change you see, the more you will want to practice!

Affirmation

Expanding our skills always requires practice. Whether its riding a bike, learning a new language or something new on the computer, it is only when we repeatedly engage our skills that we gain confidence. Say ten times, "I am joyfully committing to practicing being awake in my parenting! I know that my whole family, including me, will reap the rewards for my practice! " Repeat this throughout the day.

Self-Observation

Whether we know it or not, our lives are full of commitments. We make commitments at work, at home and with our friends. Notice where you are making your commitments. Are they worthy of the time you are putting into them? Would you rather be engaged in something else? Record your observations in your journal.

Practice

Go back through the practices presented in the previous chapters, or if you are reading this book again in any chapter you like, and pick a practice that you decided not to engage but you felt like could be helpful. Engage that practice for the week knowing that doing so will bring you closer to being a more awake, compassionate parent!

PART II: PURPOSE

Chapter 9: Find Your Own Purpose

"First say to yourself what you would be; and then do what you have to do."

~ Epectetus

During the NAZI occupation of Germany, a young psychologist named Victor Frankl was imprisoned in the Turkheim concentration camp. He was separated from his wife and family. In the midst of the horror of the camp, he noticed that some people managed to survive much longer than others. Some shared their morsels of food taking care of fellow prisoners and others just gave up. His curiosity as to what made one man go on in terrible circumstances and others give up probably kept him alive. He began to talk with his fellow prisoners and realized that what kept them alive was a sense of purpose. For some it was to rejoin their family, for others to write a book, or to follow a dream. The reason wasn't as important as their commitment to something larger than themselves, a purpose worth living for.

In our crazy, stressed out experience of the world, most of don't have much time to think about the big questions like what's our purpose. We might just think about getting by from day to day, paying the bills and hoping to catch our breath. It's all we can do just to make it through the day sometimes. But when we are only focused on survival, all we get is survival. We never get a chance to move on to something bigger.

And there is something bigger for each one of us, a purpose that draws us and a song written across our hearts that beckons us to sing. One of the biggest changes you can make in your life is to get clear about your purpose and to start living into it. It is also one of the best examples you can provide for your children.

Your purpose, an expression of your life force, is too big to be about money or survival. And deep down you probably already know this is true. We don't think there is anything wrong with money. In fact, Dan and I both quite enjoy what money allows us to do in our lives. But money is simply energy, a vehicle to something else. It provides different things for different people. For some it's security, for some it's the ability to travel, for others it allows them to live in a big house. All of these are different purposes than money itself.

Being that none of us were born knowing what money even is, if we believe there is some life purpose, it must be deeper than that. Take a minute and think back. What did you dream of as a child? Do you know who you wanted to be when you grew up? Was there a secret fantasy that you had? What brought you back to it again and again? While our childhood dreams of who we might one day be might not be our ultimate purpose, they remind us of a time when we dreamed big.

Finding our life purpose is about finding a clear direction and making choices that move us towards it. Can you imagine if you took your family on a vacation and had no idea where you were going? How would you know which airport to drive to? Or which direction to drive? Which clothes to pack? Or even if it was something you might enjoy?

Most of us, at least subconsciously, have a clear sense of what our purpose is. When we are out of alignment with it we revolt, feel sick or complain. When we are in alignment with our purpose we feel energized, alive and excited. We can't wait to get to work or to school, to learn something new and to expand our abilities to meet the challenges ahead. When we are working against (or out of alignment with) our purpose, it feels like we are being suffocated. No matter how much money or awards or appreciation that we get it doesn't seem to matter. We know that our soul is suffocating.

Dr. Mihaly Csikszentmihalyi, a professor at Claremont Graduate University, is fond of talking about experiences of flow. These are the times when we completely lose ourselves in the experience. Perhaps we have been reading a book and thought only a short time has passed only to look up and realize that we have been reading for an hour or two. Or maybe time seems to slow down as it does for many athletes when they are out on the field and really in their element.

I often find this happening when I am working with a client. While I am aware of the client and the relationship, it can seem that the rest of the world disappears. In those moments all of my attention is focused on what can happen, my intuition is speaking clearly and I know what I am doing is leading to greater wellbeing and joy in both of our lives.

If you are unsure where your true purpose lies, paying attention to where you have these experiences is a powerful way to begin. All you have to find is one of these experiences. Invite it into your mind and really pay attention to it. Notice what you were doing and what was absorbing you. Then simply invite your subconscious mind to show you other experiences that have had the same quality. They usually just pop to mind if not in this moment then later. As you examine these experiences, a pattern may begin to emerge.

Take a minute right now and ask yourself, on a scale of 1 to 10, how alive are you? How vital, enthusiastic and excited are you to wake up every morning? If you aren't able to say that you are at a 10 or 100% alive, you are likely out of alignment with your true purpose. Is that an example that you want your children to follow? Can you imagine if they decided they would simply accept being 50 or 60 percent alive? The rest of the time they would just go through the motions. It's easy for them to do that when they see adults all around them offering this example.

Imagine how life could change if you were clear about your purpose. Even as a small child I had a big sense of working to make the world a better place. I have served in non-profits and churches either paid or volunteer for most of my adult life. Now I lead workshops, write, consult and coach people in their process of waking up.

I didn't start off with a clear statement of purpose. I grew into my purpose as I learned new skills, met people who challenged me to grow and continued to travel my own developmental path. Most of this came from following what brought me to life. At this point in my life, I've come to realize that my purpose is to support human development and achievement. The more that I align my thoughts, words and actions with this goal, the more I connect to my sense of purpose and wake up to myself.

There is no requirement for our purpose to be big. I have seen people come up with beautifully simple purpose statements like, "My purpose is to love myself and others as fully as I can." But I do think that our purpose must be worthy. That it be big enough to fill our lives, to stretch us and to make us strive for something greater. You will know that your sense of purpose is big enough for you when it plucks the strings of your heart, when it resonates deeply within you and you are able to give it your full yes! You know it's right when you can see it clearly as if it is at the top of a mountain and you are moving boldly forward feeling deep in your bones that the path you are traveling is the right one.

Of course, hearing that yes requires that we can turn down the voice of fear. Sometimes all of the "what ifs" can drown out what's really most important to us with noise. The little voice in our head, the voice that diminishes us, tears us down and makes us smaller might tell us that having a big goal sets ourselves up for failure. Or perhaps challenges us. Who are we to think we could do something big in the world? But who are any of the great people of the world who decide to make a difference in big and small ways everyday? Simple humans making simple choices to show up differently, to wake up and live in the fullness of who they are. Marianne Williamson wrote,

"Our deepest fear is not that we are inadequate. Our deepest fear is that we are powerful beyond measure. It is our light, not our darkness that most frightens us. We ask ourselves, who am I to be brilliant, gorgeous, talented, fabulous? Actually, who are you not to be? You are a child of God. Your playing small does not serve the world. There is nothing enlightened about shrinking so that other people won't feel insecure around you. We are all meant to shine, as children do. We were born to make manifest the glory of God that is within us. It's not just in some of us; it's in everyone. And as we let our own light shine, we unconsciously give other people permission to do the same. As we are liberated from our own fear, our presence automatically liberates others."

There is a worthy purpose for all of us, something that is uniquely ours to do that comes out of who we are. And once we find it, it can motivate us to move mountains if we are willing to let it. Can you imagine if Martin Luther King Jr. had chosen not to deliver his "I Had a Dream" speech or if Rosa Parks had not sat down on a bus in Montgomery, Alabama? Perhaps our work is not to change the world but we never know how far our actions ripple out into the world.

Once we find our sense of purpose, we may want to guard it like a highly fragile secret. But it will only gain strength with action. Even small actions will bring your purpose vitality. Sharing this sense of purpose with your partner and your children gives them permission to have a purpose of their own that they can live into.

And it is not just individuals that have a sense of purpose. Families do as well. Have you ever thought about sitting down with your family and discussing what your family purpose is? What can you bring into the world? If you haven't done this yet, consider how much you could teach your children by engaging this process. Our world often employs busyness in place of purpose. Creating clear opportunities for children to discuss and engage in what they hope for provides a powerful impetus for a better world!

Affirmation

We all have a deep sense of purpose to wake up to in the world. Repeat the following phrase ten times now letting it come from your heart as much as you can. "I am gratefully waking up to my truest, deepest sense of purpose everyday! I know that every action, no matter the size, strengthens my purpose!" Think of this through the rest of the day.

Self-Observation

We may have to start paying attention to what brings us life. We are so busy that we miss what's really important to us. But you can take the time to notice where your heart is affirming you. Start to notice what it is that brings you joy, passion and aliveness. Keep a list. When you reach 20 or 30, see if there are any patterns. Use your observations to complete the practice.

Practice

1. Imagine what you would do if you had all the money in the world. What would bring you the most joy? Give yourself permission to be really speak from your heart.

    _____

    _____

    _____

    _____

    _____

2. When you look at your list of things that bring you life, which are actions, things like singing, dancing, or laughing? Of these, and any you choose to add, which forms of aliveness would you employ to bring about what you really want to be about in the world?

    _____

    _____

    _____

    _____

3. Form this into a purpose statement. For example, my purpose

is to write books that inspire people while loving my family, enjoying my friends, and eating great food. There's no right or wrong here.

_____

_____

_____

_____

_____

4. Put this statement in a place that you will be reminded of it frequently. Do one thing that would set you in the direction of living your purpose today!

Chapter 10: Dedicate Yourself to Life

"Dedication involves making the space to let young ideas take hold; every tree was once a seed and every company was once an idea."

~Zephyr Bloch-Jorgensen

What's the first thought that crosses your mind when the alarm clock goes off in the morning? "Coffee? I'm late? Another day?" Do you direct your thoughts in these early morning hours before you wake up your children and greet the day or do you just let them happen? Just as you can make a choice as to how you experience the world, you can also begin each day by setting your internal navigational system towards what's really important to you.

Have you ever woken up on the wrong side of the bed? You know what I mean. You feel crabby, tired and you know before you even put your feet on the floor that there is nothing that will go right. Then other days, you wake up and you feel full of energy, focused and fully alive. Sometimes there are conditions that support the mood you wake up with. You slept really well or not at all. You were worried about your presentation at work the next day or you felt secure that everything was done. You feel loved or you don't. No matter what the circumstance, you can choose a direction that is as distinct as going north or south on the highway just by dedicating your day.

"But it's too early to do anything but survive, to make it through the morning?" you might say. Or, "I'm not a morning person." But imagine this. If every morning on your commute to work you went fifty miles in the wrong direction before you really woke up, had a cup of coffee and decided to turn around, you would probably not be loving all the extra time that you spent on the road. This is how many of us live our lives. The unintentional actions that we engage in create more messes for us, requiring more effort to resolve, than just setting ourselves in the right direction in the first place.

This doesn't have to be a complicated practice. Every morning when I wake up, before I even jump out of bed, I offer a dedication of my day. The words change from day to day but usually they are something like this, "Thank you God for another day." (There's nothing that guarantees any of us will wake up in the morning so when we do, why not be thankful? While you're there, you might even offer thanks that your children are still here and you get another day to be in deeper relationship with them.) "May everything I think, say and do move the world and myself towards greater love, compassion, kindness and hope." In the process, I let myself feel grateful. For me this feels like a literal opening of the heart. It's a small practice that takes no more than a minute but it sets the direction of my day. Then I'm headed north towards my purpose and not causing collateral damage until I truly wake up.

Historically, it was not uncommon at all for people to offer a dedication for what they were doing. They were dedicating their labor to the village so that everyone could eat. They were building the cathedral or the temple to glorifying their god. When we wake up, groan and hope that we make it through the day, we are dedicating our day simply to survival. And while surviving is preferable to not, obviously, it isn't an inspiring direction to go.

A dedication practice, whether it be in the morning to put your day in order or every day before you sit down at your computer at work, honors a place in your heart that we call "sacred." It is the place where the things that are most precious to us reside like our loves, our passions and our dreams. Imagine if every morning at work, you choose to dedicate your work to your children that they might have a better life and to yourself that you would be more joyful. Can you imagine how your work would change?

Take a moment and just imagine what would happen if you dedicated your thoughts, actions and words with the people around you to bringing peace and joy to your life and theirs. Or what if you dedicated your day to connecting to the Earth and all the creatures on it or protecting children. No matter what you dedicate your time to, offering yourself in this way deepens your experience of life.

The dedication that I offer in the morning fits into my sense of purpose. What might work for you to dedicate your day, your parenting and your work? What thoughts, words and actions are you engaged in that you wouldn't want to let into that sacred space of your heart? Are they serving you?

When we discussed purpose earlier, we said that every action we take towards our deepest purpose strengthens it. Often life gets in the way of taking any action that moves us in this direction. Our autopilot, as I have noted, is set to survival mode. But when we set our autopilot to purpose mode, it increases our level of awareness so that we notice opportunities to engage the world that allow us to open into purpose.

For example, if I woke up in the morning with the thought of simply getting by, I might have breakfast, read the latest news online and go about my business none the wiser of all the opportunities before me to step into life. I would have missed the opportunity to practice gratitude for my breakfast that comes to me with the aid of so many hands. I might have missed events in the paper that inform the work that I am doing. And I might not even notice the morning passing.

In all of our lives, when we choose to firmly set our direction in line with our purpose, opportunities arise that will allow us to move forward. In fact, your next opportunity to strengthen your resolve is only an arm's length away. You simply need to look with the right lenses. If you are uncertain, simply start the day with a request, putting your mind on notice, that you see the next step that you need to take in order to make your purpose a reality. If you let your intuition partner with your resolve, you will be amazed at the opportunities that will arise.

This is an incredible opportunity to teach your children about resolve and being open to opportunities arising. If you have a family purpose of being connected to each other and the world, for example, your children will begin to see all sorts of ways that you can do this as a family. You may often miss many of these because they are not at your "eye level." These can show up in small ways, such as a way that one sibling can be kind to another sharing toys or helping with a task, or they can happen in larger ways such as when families decide to take a family vacation that is service-based rather than entertainment-based. The world is full of opportunities to move forward with your purpose when you allow yourself to see them. Dedication is the simplest way to lean into these opportunities!

Affirmation

Dedication is the practice of continually reminding yourself to follow the path that you are on. When you've found a worthy purpose you want to pursue reminding yourself that there are opportunities opening up to do so in every moment can nurture your dream. Say the following affirmation ten times and throughout the day. "I am joyfully placing myself firmly in line with my purpose. I am seeing all of the ways that I can move forward in my purpose today!"

Self-Observation

This week, simply watch out for opportunities to support your purpose. Don't let your critic take hold here. If you see an opportunity that seems out of your reach for financial or educational or whatever reason, pay it no heed. Remember these can be very small or very big. Write a list of these in your journal.

Practice

For every day that you are observing what opportunities are opening themselves up choose one action, the size of which is unimportant, that will move you toward your goal and do it. For each action that you engage, no matter how large or small, you will be building a momentum to carry you toward your purpose!

Chapter 11: Visualize Change

"What the mind can conceive and believe it can achieve."

~ Napoleon Hill

You can have a radically different relationship with your family and yourself. As you try on this idea, can you imagine what that might look like, how your conversations would shift, even how it would feel in your body to hold less stress and tension?

Take a moment now just to close your eyes and imagine the ways that you want to relate to your children. Imagine spending time with them the way you would like and feeling good about your interactions. Experience yourself parenting with great skillfulness, love and compassion. Imagining yourself acting in new ways imprints these behaviors in your subconscious mind allowing them to happen with more ease in your life.

This is a skill that Olympic athletes, world-class musicians and some of the most successful business people in the world have all developed. Many of them have employed a mental technique called visualization to improve the quality of their performance on the field, on stage and in the business world. While there are a number of successful visualization techniques, they all come down to the simple practice of rehearsing what you would like to happen in your mind before it happens. Many of my clients are initially skeptical when I suggest this technique. However, with a little practice, it soon becomes one of the staples of their visionary living toolbox.

Let's spend a minute understanding how this works and how it might affect your relationship with your children. We know from very sophisticated brain scans that when you imagine something happening your brain can't tell the difference between you imagining an event and it actually happening. Of course, you know that you are imagining it, but almost all of the neurons that would fire if you were actually doing the activity fire when you are imagining it. This works like a rehearsal for a play. Even though the audience isn't present, the performance is no less real.

We all know that practice makes perfect, or at least makes us more comfortable engaging a skill. Visualization provides an incredibly safe way for you to practice a new skill.

One of my clients was having a horrible time approaching people. He was constantly worried that they were not going to want to talk to him, that he wouldn't know the right thing to say or that he would seem inane. For an independent contractor who relies on himself to advertise, this was seriously dampening new business coming in. I asked him to practice visualizing himself meeting new people in a social setting of his choice. He was to imagine shaking the hand of the new person, looking in their eyes, introducing himself and enjoying a very comfortable conversation. He was to see the other person smiling and laughing and experience himself feeling good about the interaction.

In about two weeks he went to a huge professional conference that would have usually caused serious anxiety. He returned from the conference beaming. He had been able to comfortably make new connections with people without moving into his usual panic mode. Of course he could! He had become an old pro at meeting new people as far as his mind was concerned and he had rewired the old panic neural pathway that connected to meeting new people into one of comfort and ease.

This technique proves helpful for families in all different settings. Whether you are trying to learn a new skill or dealing with conflict, visualization can provide an entry point. Much of what we suggest throughout this book can be new and scary. It's easy for the danger signals to go off, to believe that you can't possibly do what we are suggesting.

Take a minute and prove to yourself the possibility of something greater. Close your eyes, get comfortable and do this mini-visualization exercise. For most people, two minutes or so is all this takes but spend as much time as you need to feel complete. Practice visualizing yourself successful and joyfully completing any of the exercises in the book. As in any visualization, you will want to draw in as many of your senses as possible. This will create a stronger imprint in the subconscious mind. Imagine the impact that these exercises will create in your life as you shift your relationship with yourself, your spouse and your children. The mere act of seeing yourself doing them well and feeling good about them sets up an expectation in your mind that the next time you do them you will have a similar experience. Why wouldn't you? You've already proven to your mind that you are capable.

Now that you've proved to yourself that you can do this, let's take it to the next level and apply it to your family life. Take a moment now and pick a situation where you are expecting things not to turn out well. You might be unsure what will happen or how you will react. Simply imagine this situation in as much detail as you can. The more sensory input you can provide like the smells, or the sounds, the things that you see, the more firmly imprinted this practice becomes. Give yourself five minutes and just imagine that everything that can go right does. You arrive early, you are greeted with ease, you know just what to say, and you are comfortable and calm throughout. Let yourself feel really good about all that is happening. If there are fears that come up, or the little voice that doubts you, simply let it know that you will hear from it in five minutes but not right now. When you are done check in with how you feel. Are you feeling calm? Excited? Nervous? No matter what happens in the actual situation, the more you practice your own sense of calm and ease in it, you will be able to react in a more balanced way. Of course you can, your mind will be convinced that you are an old pro at this!

Families often benefit greatly from using visualization in areas of conflict. We have lots of old stories we rehearse around conflict. They could be called our defense systems. When we know that there is a conflict, our antennae go up and we get ready for attack. Have you ever completely misunderstood what someone was saying in the midst of a situation like this? With our families, when we prepare for attack, we create a much higher possibility that we will mishear them and overreact. It's easy to get down on ourselves that we have these old stories but at one point in our lives, these defenses served us well. We just don't need them anymore. There is no shame in this. Simply appreciate the positive intention behind them and release them as they are no longer serving you.

In order to retrain those neural pathways so that you can stay calm in the midst of a difficult conversation with your family, you can use visualization. First, decide what you really would like to see happen. You probably have something important that you would like to say to your child and you would like them to hear it. They may have some needs of their own or things that they need you to hear. So what if your goal was to have an interaction where everyone's needs got addressed and the safety and wellbeing of the family was strengthened in the process. Take a minute now to formulate your own outcome.

Now that you know what you would like to create with your children, begin to create that possibility by imagining it five minutes a day for about two weeks. In order to get the most neural pathways you can involved you want to add as much sensory detail as possible. So, for example, simply close your eyes and imagine that you are going into your child's room. You see the posters on the wall, the color of the bedspread, call to detail every thing that you can. Now imagine you are talking with your child in a calm and loving way. They clearly hear that you are concerned and that your goal is to support them in growing up into happy people. You are completely open to listening to everything that they have to say, to really understanding what they are going through and coming up with solutions that work for everyone. Imagine that you come to a positive resolution, you hug and you know that you love each other deeply.

You may say, "No way, Jose. That will never work with my kid. You just don't know them." And we don't need to. This technique has worked with clients in all kinds of situations with all kinds of people. It works because the goal is not to control the other person. The goal is to create an openness and ease in yourself. Knowing that it takes one person reacting to what another says to fight, in this example you are practicing remaining calm, knowing that these difficult conversations are a time for you to grow and to express your love for your child.

It takes repetition because most of us have been living one set of behavioral patterns most of our lives. Your old neural pathways are deep and automatic. Each time that you mentally rehearse staying calm in difficult situations, you retrain your brain so that it goes to the new behavior rather than the old one.

This technique is not just for people who tend to get angry in conflict, it also works if your tendency is to retract or shut down during a conflict. If you are someone who swallows your words and doesn't say what's important, this is also a form of reaction. It's usually rooted in fear that someone won't love you or will get angry with you if you speak your truth. You can create new neural pathways in yourself simply by practicing the same pattern as you saw in the first example. Imagine how you would like to respond. You say what you need to in a way that the other person can hear you. You are calm and confident. You know that what you have to say is important and saying it will allow you to be in closer relationship and let you live more true to yourself.

And it's not just about conflict. We've started there because places that cause anxiety are the most common entry points to visualization. You can use this technique anywhere you would like to practice a new way of being. Mentally practice being more kind to people at work, more assertive with your boss, gentler with your partner. Whatever you would like to invite into your life, when you imagine it, you create the neural pathways to make it happen.

This is a powerful and easy technique to teach your children and it can radically alter their levels of anxiety as well as increase their sense of possibility and self-confidence. Think back to when you had to give reports in school or take tests. If these ever caused you anxiety, it is unlikely that you had a tool that would help you ease into this. You probably gritted your teeth and just got through it. But you can help your children learn a different path by simply imagining that they are in their classroom. They are sitting down to take the test. They are feeling calm and peaceful and they know all the answers. They can see themselves filling in the test and feeling confident. They are able to remember everything that they have learned and communicate in a clear way for the teacher to understand. If your child enjoys sports, you can teach them this tool to imagine sinking the ball in the hoop or crossing the finish line. If they play a musical instrument, you can teach them to imagine performing their music flawlessly, comfortably, knowing every note and feeling good about their performance

It doesn't really matter where children initially use this tool, once they know that it is something that helps them succeed in life, they will be able to refer back to it. It might even be that you are nervous about trying to teach your child something like this. Simply visualize being open to them, expressing your interest, showing them how it works and them receiving it well and you feeling good about the process.

Drawing from the world of ancient Greek philosophy, Steven Covey, the noted organizational expert, likes to say that creation happens first in the mind then in the world. Visualization gives you a chance to be a creator first in your mind and then allow the physical reflection of this creation to appear!

Affirmation

The imagination is one of the most powerful tools we have to work with our patterns of behavior. It helps us reprogram our conditioned neural responses and create new patterns. Experiment with the following affirmation ten times. "I am harnessing the power of my imagination to bring more joy and balance into my life. I know I can create in my life what I can see in my mind!" Say it to yourself throughout the day.

Self-Observation

For the next few days notice where you might feel like you are not getting your needs met. How would you prefer this situations go? Write this down.

Practice

Pick one of the recurring instances that you noticed and create a visualization practice for it. It will help your visualization practice if it is rooted in everyone getting their needs met. Remember to be as specific as you can be and to imagine things going as you would like. Spend five minutes doing this everyday for two weeks and see what happens.

Remember the basics of visualization as you engage this practice:

1. Come to a resting point, calm and relaxed.

2. Focus on yourself acting in new ways.

3. Imagine others responding well.

4. Be as vivid as possible as you engage all of your senses.

Chapter 12: Set Goals to Make Change Real

"The tragedy of life doesn't lie in not reaching your goal. The tragedy lies in having no goals to reach."

~ Benjamin Mays

I drove across country a lot when I was younger. As a native Virginian who became a California graduate student, I found myself making the cross-country trek at least once and often twice a year. For much of the trip there is lush forest or beautiful mountains, great cities or rivers where you can stop and relax. And then there are long stretches of nothingness in states like Texas, Kansas and Iowa. Depending on the route you take, you can go hours and hours with not much but cornfields or deserts as your companion. In these periods, it is essential to have a concrete goal as to where you might land next. When you finally do arrive at the next town, you can celebrate that you made it and know that you are that much closer to your destination.

Just about every business knows that in order to sustain a big vision, there have to be milestones along the way. When they are setting out to reach their purpose, they build in signposts that tell them how far they have gone. Rarely do families have goals like this. I know my family didn't growing up. Once you have adopted a family purpose, your whole family can set goals together that will help you reach your destination. You can also set goals for yourself on your own journey.

No matter what dynamic that you are seeking to invite into your family, if you have years and years of practicing something else, it will take time to release the old and bring in the new. Changing your relationship with your family, especially when you have a long history of upset, can be a difficult journey.

One of the ways to know that this trip is proceeding in the right direction is to set some concrete goals along the way. You are probably already doing this in other areas of your life. You have sales goals to meet at the office, you have budget goals to meet at home and your children may even have goals for their report cards. But what would happen if you set some concrete goals for the way that you will relate to your family? And what if your whole family got together to set some goals for how you might like to relate to each other?

What might this look like? Well, concrete goals are generally things that you can measure. In our experience, there are certain signs that some shift is happening, ways that behavior patterns change. Let's say that you have decided you want to spend more time with your children. This is great but it's too vague to serve as a goal. You have to ask yourself what spending more time with your children looks like. Will you eat dinner together twice a week? Will you read them a bedtime story four nights a week? Will you set up a special family day once a month where everyone gets together to play games or go on an adventure?

As well as asking what meeting your goal might look like, you want to ask yourself what it might feel like. You could easily spend more time with your children watching TV and it might not feel like you are even in the same house. Or you could have more family dinners together but they could be filled with fighting or chilly silence. So ask yourself what flavor or emotional tone you want as well. You are aiming to come up with a goal like "eating dinner with my family three nights a week where we enjoy being together and can talk to each other freely."

As you set your goal, you might also ask yourself whether your goal is the same goal as the other members of your family? And if not, is there is a way to achieve what you are trying to in a way that makes room for everyone? So, for example, let's say that your daughter loves theater and is in the school play. Rehearsals are several nights a week and in order to have your family dinners together she would have to miss rehearsals. It is unlikely in this case that you will get a daughter who enjoys being together if she is missing out on engaging her passion. This is a great place to engage the whole family. You can share with them your desire to spend more family time together and ask what their ideas might be. Having your whole family set goals together is much more likely to bring about what you would like and they may think of opportunities to reach this goal that you didn't imagine. What if instead of family dinners you had family rehearsals where you helped your daughter learn her lines? So perhaps you would set a goal as a family to have dinner together two nights a week and to all run lines together once a week where everyone enjoys being together. Even better is that you have helped your children learn how to express their needs, look for ways to meet them and set goals.

Goals are ways to see progress happening and help you along your journey. They are not meant to shame you if you don't reach them but rather to provide some feedback as to whether you are parenting the way you want to. One of my favorite sayings is there is no failure only feedback. When you don't reach your goals, you have an opportunity to see what feedback you are receiving and how you can shift your actions so that you can achieve what you desire.

The power of goals is not in whether we reach them. It's whether we stretch ourselves in the attempt. I advise my clients to reach beyond what is safe. To set goals for themselves that would help them grow as a human being.

Coach and teacher Chris Howard offers a powerful set of criteria to CREATE goals that work. He uses the letters of the word create to provide a helpful reminder as you build your goal.

First, be **clear and concise.** Your goal statement needs to be only a sentence of two. Often, when I ask people to define a particular goal, they can go on and on. It becomes easy for them and me to get lost in the details and miss the actual goal. So just keep it simple.

Second, be **realistic** in your goal. Your goal should be something that is achievable. I am not suggesting that you aim low here but rather you figure out what is possible. If a middle-aged man came to me and told me he wanted to be an astronaut for NASA, we would face the obstacle of him being way past the age limit for that program. We want to pick goals that will be within the realm of possibility.

For most people this is fairly simple. You can ask yourself what you could have in your relationship that would allow you to feel happier, more resourceful and full of joy. This could be as simple as the capacity to listen more or to learn greater patience. And always feel free to dream big. If someone else can do it, you know that a path has been laid and you can follow it. If they haven't done it, you can learn from all the trail blazers who have gone places where others have not been before.

Third, be **ecological**. You want to make sure that the goal that you set fits into the rest of your life and does no harm to anyone else or the planet.   If your goal harms others, not only will there be significant resistance to it, you will also be sacrificing lots of opportunities to work with others to move forward in life.

Fourth, imagine your goal **as if** it is happening right now. You want your goal to be present tense oriented so that you are imagining your goal showing up in your life right this minute.

Fifth, put it in **time**.   When you visualize your goal happening, you want to give it a specific time.   I want to firmly plant it on my future timeline so that I am constantly working towards it.   For example, you might say, "It is October 4, 2012 and I'm standing at the pyramids of Egypt happy that I have fulfilled my lifelong dream."   If your goal is vague or has phrases like "Next month I will..." then chances are your goal will continually be pushed into the future.

The criteria of as is and time can sometimes be a bit confusing to clients.   It's actually less complicated than it sounds. You want to be able to imagine yourself on a concrete date in the future acting as if your goal is happening in that moment.   When we talk about that moment, we keep it in the present tense to remind ourselves what it will feel like.   If it still seems a little confusing, simply try the form out and you will find that it makes sense.

Finally, include a form of **evidence** that you have accomplished your goal right in the goal statement itself. For example, if you want to lose weight, the evidence might be seeing the scale at the weight that you want to be. If you wanted to earn more money, the evidence might be seeing yourself depositing checks into the bank or looking at your balance online and seeing it go up. This is the step that shows that you have accomplished the goal fully.

Howard suggests using the following format for framing your goals. I have found this construction really helpful with clients since it's easy to put together and remember.

Formula for goals: It is now _____ (future date), I am/ I have _____ (evidence).

Let's look at a few examples.   These are some goals of the clients I have worked with in the past.

- It is October 1, 2009. I am standing on my scale seeing that I weigh 150 pounds and I am excited that I have reached my goal.

- It is June 5, 2008. I am reading my children a bedtime story for the fourth night in a row happy to be spending the time I want with them.

- It's February 4, 2007. I am turning in the final draft of my dissertation feeling good that I have taken a big step towards completing my Ph.D.

You can easily construct your own goal statement using the formula and the examples above.

It is also helpful to track your goals in a way that can show you progress. It doesn't have to be complicated. Perhaps on your calendar you note whether or not you read a story to your child that day. At the end of the week you can tally these up and see if you reached your goal. Tracking your progress continually brings awareness to what you want to accomplish. Remember, whatever you pay attention to will increase in your life.

Our goals are our conscious declarations of where we intend to go in our lives. Each movement towards these goals, no matter how big or small, brings them one step closer. The more energy that you bring to your hopes, your dreams, and your best intentions with your children, the more likely they are to become reality!

Self-Observation

By now you have defined a sense of purpose for yourself and you have a vision for your family. Notice what might be the goals that are in line with that sense of purpose. Write these in your journal.

Practice

Use the formula for creating goals that we have explained in this chapter to write out a few specific goals that will help you move towards your purpose. Remember to allow your goals to be concise, realistic, ecological, framed in present tense/"as if" language, connected to a certain timeframe and clear about the evidence it will take for you to know you have accomplished the goal.

For the following week spend two or three minutes a day imagining into your goal as if it you were standing in that moment and your goal was accomplished. Do whatever it takes to make it feel as real as possible.

Affirmation

Once we have a clear goal, it isn't unusual to find all kinds of ways to move that goal forward that we never dreamed of. Perhaps someone will offer you help or you will hear of a new opportunity. You may find a book that would be useful to read. Once you've set your goal, it is like raising your antenna so that you notice more ways to meet it. Allow you affirmation practice to support your goal. You can simply say ten times a day, "I am open to new opportunities to assist me in reaching my goal. I am constantly seeing new ways to move forward and allowing them to propel me forward."

Chapter 13: Build Momentum for Change

"Follow your bliss and the universe will open doors for you where there were only walls."

~ Joseph Campell

I am really fortunate to have some pretty amazing people come to me for coaching. It often feels like a gift that I get to witness the transformations that happen in their lives. But you would be surprised how often when they arrive they are completely immobilized. Even when they have a strong sense of purpose and they have a goal, they may not be moving forward. For a lot of these folks, they haven't figured out that they don't have to be perfect or do it all at once to create change in their lives. All a person has to do is begin.

I had an amazing young woman come to work with me a few years ago. She was smart and talented, had lots of education and when she walked into a room, you could see people light up. She was so easy to like. And she was feeling completely suffocated.

She was living at home, working at a job she didn't enjoy and not really employing her creative spirit. (She was quite an amazing artist.) She set the intention of creating more spaciousness in her life. She wasn't sure what that would mean in her life but she knew that she wanted that feeling.

She began by making very small changes. She made a point to take a walk during her lunch break. She asked for small changes to be made in her living situation that would make it easier for her. And she began to find small ways to take care of herself better. Within a year, these small steps had led to her finding an apartment of her own, starting her own successful consulting business and feeling truly alive.

No matter what you would like to create with your family, no matter how much change you want to make, it all starts with a single step forward. And you have been stepping the whole way through this book! Every page that you have read in this book, every conversation that you have had about its contents, and every one of the exercises that you have engaged have been building a new momentum towards awake parenting.

Many of us look at how big the task ahead is and get absolutely overwhelmed. We simply freeze in the face of the challenge. When I was writing my dissertation, I came upon this challenge. While you learn quite a bit in graduate school, no one ever really teaches you how to write a book. When it came time to write my dissertation, I had read lots of books, written lots of papers, and even taught quite a few university classes. But asking me to write a 200 page book left me feeling like I had been asked to empty the ocean with a teaspoon. The task simply seemed too big for me.

Then one of my professors suggested that I think about it as eight forty page papers. I was used to writing those but still the task was daunting. Then a friend suggested that I stop being frozen and simply write a page a day, probably a thirty-minute commitment at most. "What's that going to get me?" I wondered. Well, what that got me was a completed dissertation draft in 200 days. Writing one page a day created the space to get excited about the idea. Often I didn't want to stop after that page was finished and I just kept on writing. In the end, I reached my goal, passed my defense with flying colors, and had a dissertation that I was proud of to show for it.

If our goals are big enough to make us stretch, chances are they can also seem to be daunting at times. But sitting still on the side of the road complaining about the long journey ahead never got anyone anywhere. Only by putting one foot in front of the other, no matter how slowly, will we move ahead a little at a time until we eventually reach our goal. When we know what our purpose is and we have dedicated our work to those we love, this process becomes much easier. We have something to pull us towards our goal by way of our heart rather than feeling like we must muscle our way through.

And a funny thing happens on this journey. It is easy to believe that you have to do everything to achieve your goals on your own. Particularly in a frozen spot, we can feel like we are the only ones who are really trying to do something with our lives, that there are no resources to support us and no one really seems to care. Fortunately, when we start to move forward we notice that there are fellow travelers on the road with us. When we raise our heads high and are able just to look around us, we see that there is a whole army of angels who want to support us in reaching our goal. And part of building our forward going momentum is to accept their support.

Becoming a more awake parent can feel like a daunting goal. Often clients feel like there is so much that they need to change. They have inherited old scripts from their parents that they want to erase. They have been engaged in unskillful habits that they want to replace. It can seem like they are never going to get to the Promised Land. And they can feel like their particular damaging by their parents leaves them alone in the universe with no one to turn to. But there are people all over the world who, out of love for themselves and their children, are looking for ways to become more awake parents. When you begin this work, you enter a community of people that are supporting each other and themselves on a journey to a new world, a land that has not yet been completely discovered. On that journey, parents share stories with each other, tools, heartbreaks, tears and laughter. Relationships are built and everyone becomes better for it in the process.

Take a minute right now to acknowledge all the movement that you already have made. Just by reading this book, you are moving forward. Even if it's at a snail's pace, you are not standing still. You have opened your heart to a new possibility and you are creating something new in this moment.

Now ask yourself who has already provided support on this journey and who is waiting to provide more when you are ready to receive it. You are getting support from the authors of this book just in the ideas and practices you are receiving. Perhaps your partner, your friends or your relatives have provided support. And if you feel no support simply breathe deeply and ask your higher wisdom to show you where there is support in your life that you have not yet seen. It will show up just for the asking!

Movement is happening as we speak. But sometimes we resist it as if someone is pushing us gently from behind and we tense our bodies to resist the effort. You can always choose the pace at which you move in your life. And often, when you are ready, all you have to do is stop resisting and allow yourself to move with the support and momentum that have already been built up in your life.

Who knows if any of us will reach our goals? All we can really do is try. What we do know is that every time you have an interaction with a child you wouldn't have otherwise, every time you hear an "I love you" from the heart, every time your child comes to you with a problem because they trust you to be supportive, you know that the journey is worth every step whether you get to the end or not. Be proud of yourself for engaging this journey. You have already done more than you know and there is so much more waiting for you for the taking.

Affirmation

Every step that you take leads you further along your path to awake parenting. Repeat the following affirmation ten times now and throughout the day. "I am joyfully building powerful momentum as I become a more awake parent. Every step I take moves me closer to my goals!"

Self-Observation

For the next few days just notice all the places that you can support yourself in moving forward in your life. What supports exist around you? What friends, family and resources can you draw on? If you are having a hard time seeing these, just breathe deeply and ask that your inner wisdom show you where these supports are. Make a list in your journal.

Practice

Sometimes it's hard to see all the progress we have made in the middle of the journey. We look towards the goal and can't see all that we have accomplished. Make a list of all the things that have already put in motion. Then visualize yourself moving joyfully forward with the momentum that already is there for you the minute you stop resisting it.

PART III: PRESENCE

Chapter 14: Empty Yourself to Receive

"Even God can't fill what's already full."

~ Mother Theresa

"We too should make ourselves empty, that the great soul of the universe may fill us with its breath."

~ Lawrence Binyon

"The universe is made of stories, not of atoms."

~Muriel Rukeyser

I came to coaching with a central question that I have still not resolved. I want to know why we aren't all living joyful, brilliant, loving lives. So I ask a lot of people what is stopping them from doing what they really would love to do in their lives? Sometimes they tell me it's about money or lack of education or some other thing that they are lacking. These are relatively easy to fix if they want to because things can almost always be acquired.

The more entrenched blocks are the stories that people tell about themselves. They usually start off with something like, "I'm just too shy, too dumb, too weak, too _____ (add your own)." These are all stories people tell themselves everyday. We all tell these stories. Stories are the way that we make sense of our lives from one seemingly random event to the next.

Working with parents, it is often their stories of childhood that hold them back. We have heard parents tell stories like, "I am not patient or wise or loving." At the base of these stories is the tale that they are not enough and probably never will be. We often inherit these stories from our childhood and because they've been with us for so long, they can become almost impossible to see. What we can't see can be very difficult to change. For that reason, bringing our stories to light is a very important piece of the process of waking up.

There are three characteristics that these stories all share. First, they define what we see. When we look out at the world, if the story that we are telling is that we are a victim, we will only see the ways in which we have been a victim. We will miss all the times that we have been a hero, taken charge and been responsible for our own lives.

Second, they are the primary way that we relate to people, places and events. No matter what story we are telling, we will relate to people as if they are playing a role in it. If you are telling a story that no one ever meets your needs, then no matter who enters your life and what they do, they will never be able to meet your needs. You have already written the story and there is no room for anyone to be an independent agent in it. To allow someone to do otherwise would require you to rewrite your story.

Third, these stories are largely invisible to us. For most of us, these stories get established when we are children. They are our means of understanding the world that we are living in. So if your parents were overprotective, you might tell a story that says you are weak and can't take care of yourself. If your parents were not able to meet your needs, you might tell a story that says others don't see you or that your needs can't be met, so why bother? As interpretations of life events, these stories always start out with a lie that we have made true. While our parents might not have known how to meet our needs, others in our lives, including ourselves, can now do that. If they taught us that we were frail and needed to be taken care of, we can also find a thousand ways that we have been strong and independent.

These stories quickly trap us into seeing the world and ourselves through a lens of exaggerated limitation. We and the world become smaller and less capable. Then we pass these stories onto the people in our lives, to partners, to children, to friends and even to enemies. Without knowing what these stories are, your children become part of an inherited set of stories from your parents.

Even when we know these stories aren't serving us, they can be very difficult to let go of. They have become good friends to us, companions that have told us that we have done nothing wrong, that we are victims and the world has wronged us. Or they may tell us we are all bad, that nothing we do goes right and that it's all our fault. Even when they are not positive stories, they are comfortable in their familiarity, like a worn out chair that doesn't quite fit you but recognizes your body. They keep us locked in our smallness and fear.

When an old story is suddenly seen, it often takes all the power out of it. I remember being in an advanced coaching training a few years back and finding myself feeling like there was nothing that I had to offer. That all of the other people in the room were the "real" coaches as they had more corporate experience than I did. (Like I said, we can always find a way to make our stories true.)

Even as other people in the sessions were coming to me to understand the models that we were learning, I was not realizing my own value. Then a colleague challenged me to "ride my expertise like a horse." This image jumped into my mind and allowed me to realize how much of an old story from my own childhood that I had been viewing the training through and opened up all kinds of space for me.

That opening was a beginning and for weeks after that training I found myself noticing other places that old story was showing up. Allowing myself to non-judgmentally release the story opened up boldness in my coaching and now some of my favorite people to coach are other coaches. And anytime I start to tell that old story, I simply remember the words, "Hi ho Silver away!"

There is an old Southern expression that says, "the devil you know is better than the devil you don't." It points to the fact that we at least know how to be in relationship with the devil, or the old stories of smallness and hurt that can fill our hearts and minds, that we have experienced in our lives. When we release them, we can be afraid of what might come to take their place. And what if nothing comes to take their place? Will we be all alone and have to face ourselves unprotected?

If you remember back to our first pathway of awake parenting, we get to choose our relationship to all our experiences, you know that you are choosing a relationship to that past experience that is limiting to you. This happens a lot with men who don't feel like they can be emotional around their children. They might say that their father never provided them an example of how to show their emotions. But surely other people could provide that example. Surely men exist who show their emotions, make themselves vulnerable and are role models. In fact, there is an entire men's movement doing just this.

One of the most profound things that you can do for yourself and for your children is to begin to let go of these limiting stories that you are telling yourself about your experiences as a child. This can feel like a very difficult process. We formed our childhood beliefs to make sense of our world. And they have served us in the pursuit of survival. They have accompanied us on our journey all of our lives. But it may be time to put away childhood things, release some of your stories and reframe others.

I am the last person to claim that our parents cannot be very damaging to us in our early years. Certainly many people experienced abuse of many forms as well as neglect. My only claim here is that to hold onto those beliefs in adulthood is not serving you. It is okay to thank those beliefs for their service and release them. There are better stories that can serve you now. And now that you are not small, weak and vulnerable, you can re-write your stories so they can be sources of expansion and freedom.

Take a moment and see if there are any stories or beliefs about yourself or parenting that aren't serving you and your children. The point of this is not to make your parents wrong and to say they were bad. It's simply to admit that most parents were doing the best they knew how and that they still managed to pass on beliefs and stories that do not serve us. Think about most white parents who were born before the Civil Rights movement in America. They had inherited a whole set of beliefs from their parents and their culture that told them that people of other skin tones were somehow deficient. These were clearly beliefs that needed to be released. What beliefs might you like to release?

Our stories have been with us so long that they can become like a second skin and it can be very difficult to see them. We become comfortable with our limitations and back away from them believing that encountering our boundaries may cause pain. Some folks like to do an emotional excavation of their past trying to determine all of the ways in which their parents damaged them and inventorying the wreckage that they left behind. In the end, they are still left mostly with wreckage. I prefer a more gentle process where you simply invite those beliefs that are not serving you to make themselves known to you. You will likely start to notice them as soon as you make the request. If you need help, you can ask close friends, a therapist or a coach for assistance in seeing them and for support as you release them.

As we let go of old beliefs, there is an amazing opportunity to choose which beliefs we will continue to hold. What stories do you want to tell your children about family? What beliefs would you like to pass on to them? This work of recreating is going on all over America as family has reformed to include families in all different configurations that are loving and compassionate. These include extended families, stepfamilies, as well as gay and lesbian families that are all telling a new story of what it means to be family. And we are better off for releasing the old, limiting tales that have been told to us preventing us from seeing the beauty in all of them.

This tool becomes even more powerful as you teach your children to be able to recognize the stories that they tell themselves. You can do this even when your children are very young by asking them what the story might be for characters in their favorite bedtime tales. Gregory Maguire, author of <u>Wicked</u>, asks what story would the Wicked Witch of the West tell in the Wizard of Oz. What about Glenda? The lion? The scarecrow? You can do this with any story. Ask your children what different stories they might be able to tell themselves that would change their actions.

None of us are too old or too young to examine the stories that we are imposing on the world. Letting go of these stories allows us to see the world just as it is, without all our filters and to breathe life and freedom into our experience of ourselves and the world around us.

Affirmation

Everyday we can choose a new way to look at the world. And we can release old beliefs that are not serving us. Say ten times, "I am joyfully releasing any and all stories and beliefs that no longer serve me or my purpose in life." Say this throughout the day.

Self-Observation

The stories we grow up with can be so close to us that we often can't even see them. They become like a second skin. For the next few days ask yourself what beliefs are under the actions that you take that don't serve you. Record your observations in your journal.

Practice

For those of you whose parents (and grandparents) are still alive, give them a call and ask them what learned from their parents that turned out to not serve them. What did they have to release? While you are talking with them, thank them for doing the best that they were able to, for being your parents.

In addition, you can take your list of beliefs that are not serving you and write a more life affirming belief that you would rather hold. Use the form of affirmation and repeat them to yourself ten times a day for the next week and as long beyond that as you like.

Chapter 15: Understand Your Basic Needs

"There is nothing that will not reveal its secrets if you love it enough."
~ George Washington Carver

"You want to be loved because you do not love; but the moment you love, it is finished, you are no longer inquiring whether or not somebody loves you."

~ Krishnamurti

All of life leans towards meeting our basic needs. Plants send their roots down into the soil to drink water. They send their shoots and leaves up to the sky to gather sunlight. All animals on the planet act to meet their basic needs for food, shelter and propagation. Humans also have needs that we must meet or we are not truly living. We can last a few days without water, a few weeks without food, and even years without love and still we will survive but in all of these cases, we are starving ourselves of our basic needs. Only when our basic needs are acknowledged and met can we really move to a place of joy.

In the Western world the majority of us have our physical needs met. And there actually is enough to go around for everyone to meet these needs if we begin to rethink the way we share our resources. While our physical needs require external sources, most of our emotional needs can be met internally. Meeting these needs for ourselves allows others to add to our abundance rather than be responsible for it.

Many of the parents we work with want to know why their kids are driving them crazy. They, like all of us, have gotten caught up believing that they are the center of the universe and that their kids are purposefully doing things to them. Take a minute and think back to your own childhood and adolescence. When you did things that got you into trouble with your parents, how often did your actions have anything to do with your parents? Were your actions directed at them?

Or were you only concerned with the possible consequences?

Kids of all ages, like adults, are rarely thinking much about their parents. They are living in their own drama with their own two-inch headlines. And fundamentally, they are just trying to meet their own needs. One of my favorite rules, the 18-40-60 Rule, points this out with the humor it deserves. At 18 we think everyone is paying attention to us, at 40 we don't care who is paying attention to us and at 60, we realize that everyone has been too busy thinking about themselves to pay much attention to us after all.

When your kids are driving you crazy, which can mean everything from being too loud when you'd like them to be quiet, making a mess when you want them to be cleaner, exploring illicit substances when you want them to abstain, their needs are in conflict with yours. Besides the basic survival needs that keep our bodies running, there are three basic emotional survival needs that we all long to have met. The more you are able to identify the needs that you are trying to have met as well as the needs your children are trying to meet, the more capable you are of making choices that build relationships with them.

The three basic emotional survival needs are the need to be seen, the need to belong and the need to create. All three of these can be seen as expressions of love. For the most part, our culture isn't supporting these needs being met right now. Too many commercials, TV shows, and even our larger cultural stories tell us that our needs can be met in a mall. If you can just find the right object that will fulfill your desires then you will be happy. And this plays off of our instincts as hunters and gatherers. To meet our physical needs, we know that we must search outside ourselves and eventually we can find things that do satisfy us. But this misses the very deep difference that exists between physical and emotional needs.

The first of these needs is the need to be seen and to be appreciated. In yoga classes, practitioners will often greet each other with the Hindu salutation "namaste." This basically means, "the divine in me greets the divine in you." Seeing the sacredness of the person standing in front of us is one of the ways in which we can see or acknowledge the fullness of their humanity. When children learn new skills like riding a bike or leaping, they often can't wait to show their parents what they can do and who they are becoming. They are longing to demonstrate their power and expansiveness to their parents, to be seen for the amazing beings that they are. Understanding that their efforts are not meant to disrupt your life but rather to connect deeply with you, to invite you to witness their "becoming" as they step into their own power, can help to put their demand for your time into perspective.

When we are able to offer ourselves this kind of deep attention, to meet our own need to be seen, it becomes much easier to do the same for other people as well as to allow ourselves to be seen.

I often do an exercise in workshops where I ask people to introduce themselves by the name they were given, the name others call them and the name they call themselves. Most often the name they call themselves is a True Name or at least one of them. It reflects how they would like to see themselves. What is your true name? Do you allow time to see yourself? Do you create space for others to see you or does even the thought of being seen for who you are bring up a sense of fear?

Take a moment to think about who really sees you in your life. Who knows you by your true name? Who sees the sacred in you even on your bad hair days, your messy emotional days and when you are a complete failure? Who sees the sacred in you when you are at your best, loving life and laughing freely? Do you see your children in the same way?

A while back I worked with a mother from Canada in her late thirties. She had two step-children and while she was raising them she was struggling to build a business. No matter what interventions I provided, she was constantly at the edge of exhaustion. I kept mirroring back the profound need that she had in her life for rest and self-care and working with her to find ways to meet those needs. No matter what we did, she simply couldn't find the time to meet her own needs. She was waiting for someone else to do it.

Unfortunately, her partner was also struggling. Their oldest child was just out of rehab and their youngest was demanding more and more attention. No one in the family was able to see her the way she wanted because they too were in the midst of their own dramas.

Many people spend a lifetime waiting for someone else to truly see them for who they are. They wait for a lover or a parent to reflect back what they want to hear and when the reflection comes back through the lens of the other, not exactly what they want to hear, they feel misunderstood and even resentful. Acknowledging and honoring ourselves, as if our heart was our witness, goes a long way towards meeting this basic need. Then we can begin to reveal ourselves so that others can actually see the person behind the facade that we most often project out for the world to see. It seems only fair that until we choose to be transparent, we can't be mad with others for not seeing what we won't show.

The second need is to belong, which is ultimately the desire to trust that there is something greater than ourselves. We want to be connected to people who love us whether they are friends, family or community. In an increasingly fragmented world, this can seem an almost impossible demand. We live isolated lives and our families are often thousands of miles away. Our world is impermanent and our connections all too often feel fleeting. Take a moment and reflect. Where do you belong?

One of the most common complaints I hear from new clients is that they just don't have anyone to talk to. They are missing community. Living in a big city, the four women in the popular Showtime series, "Sex in the City," often come up as an example of what people are longing for. We always seem on the lookout for the other who we can claim as our own. Those special people that we can connect to.

Take another moment and ask yourself to whom you belong? We often try to fill this with a "special" person in our lives like a partner or spouse but there are many other ways that we can belong. Who is your tribe? Do you trust that they will support you when you need them? Do your children have a sense of tribe? Of belonging? How can you support this need?

It is not surprising that studies have found people who practice some sort of religious practice tend to live longer, happier lives. Even their marriages are reported as a bit happier. In part, this is because they practice trusting in something larger than themselves. This does not need to be a particular perspective of the sacred but rather simply a deep knowing that there is something bigger than ourselves that holds us. The more we are able to trust that there is something bigger than ourselves, the less tightly we have to hold others and the more open we can become to having this need met with ease and gentleness.

The last need is to create, to make a difference, touch another heart, make contact, and leave a legacy. As humans, all that we are is longing for a way to express itself. Finding a way to do this is ultimately our work in the world. When we are lucky, this is also what we get paid for but it doesn't have to be. Do you listen to your own inner desires to create? What are they telling you? What will be your legacy for generations to come? What opportunities exist for your children to do the same?

The beginning of the work is to acknowledge our own needs and move towards fulfilling them. This means that we choose to lean into life and vitality. Our energy increases and what seemed like insurmountable blocks often seem to simply disappear, as they are no longer needed. Take a moment and do a quick self-check. On a scale of 0 to 10, ask yourself how well your needs are being met. First, think about your need to be seen. Second, your need to belong. And finally, your need to create. Then, ask yourself how your own lack is being reflected back to your children. Can you make a commitment to meeting your own needs while you are helping your children meet theirs?

Meeting our own basic needs is a vital part of supporting ourselves and our families. Helping your children understand these needs can give them greater clarity about the choices they are making in their lives. When you are able to understand that the work of children is learning how to meet their own needs, you can reframe those times when they simply aren't supporting what you want them to do. They are trying, often unskillfully, to meet their basic needs to be seen, to belong and to create. How could you help your children learn to meet their needs today? How could you move towards meeting your own needs?

Knowing that we are all trying to meet these basic needs, you can find ways to cooperate to help everyone meet their own needs. And you can also help your family adopt a much more gentle view of each other when you are skillful!

Affirmation

All of life leans towards meeting our needs. When we allow ourselves to acknowledge our needs and meet them in the most appropriate places, we feel fulfilled and alive. Repeat the following affirmation ten times now and as often as you like later. "I am becoming aware of and meeting my own needs today. As I meet my own needs, I know I have more space to help others meet theirs."

Self-Observation

Pay attention this week to people who confuse you. When your children do things that you don't really understand, ask yourself what need they are trying to meet? Use this throughout the week. Don't forget to pay attention to your own behaviors. Ask whether or not these particular behaviors are meeting the needs they aim to. Write down your observations in your journal.

Practice

This week, practice asking for the need that is most compelling in your life to be met by those that you love. Be specific about how they can fill that need. Ask yourself how you can fulfill that same need. Be specific and carry out that action.

Chapter 16: Return to Beginner's Mind

"In the beginner's mind there are many possibilities. In the expert's mind there are few."

~ *Shunryu Suzuki*

"Ideas are like rabbits. You get a couple and learn how to handle them, and pretty soon you have a dozen."

~ *John Steinbeck*

Dan and I are considered experts. We have studied long enough to have earned the highest degrees in our fields. We have done research, read widely and written thousands of pages of discourse. And everyday we are asked questions where people expect us to share our wisdom. But the greatest wisdom that either of us can impart is to simply ask questions, be still and let a person reveal themselves.

In my experience as a coach, most people actually have the answers that they are seeking. My role is to give them the time and the space to talk them out. For example, there have been many times when I have wandered all about my house looking for my glasses only to realize that I am wearing them. At other times, I've searched all over for my keys only to discover them in my pocket waiting to accompany me wherever I am going. If I were to ask you about my keys, you could tell me what you know about keys, stories of keys you have lost and you might even tell me of a time where no one really locked their doors. While all of this might be interesting, it doesn't create the space for me to find my own keys, to look in my pocket and discover I am already carrying them. Our truths often lay just below the surface waiting to have a safe enough space to emerge.

In our fast paced world, it seems that people are always demanding answers when they should really be asking questions. They want to know how the company can make more money without knowing what the company does with the money. They want to know how much the latest gadget costs without asking whether this will actually enhance their lives or simply add something else to take care of. This is, at least partly, tied up in our demand for the outside world to meet our needs. We are always looking for the next thing that will satisfy us and missing the fact that we are carrying around what we really need.

We can relate to our families in the same way. Our partner tells us about a situation at work and asks us what we think. Of course, they never seem satisfied by our reply. Perhaps this is because it doesn't fit into what they already know to be true for them. The more questions you can ask them, the more likely they can come to their own solution, to see their own truth staring back at them. But when we rush to solve, we dis-empower the other person, assuming that from our limited understanding of their life, we know the answer.

With children, especially in adolescence, asking questions can be difficult since they are still figuring themselves out. Parents often find themselves asking the frustrated question of why. Why didn't you study for the test? Why did you smoke pot with your friends? Why did you do something that you know is wrong? Of course, these are not questions that allow any space for a real response. They are just a way of expressing judgment, fear, anger and frustration. In these cases, questions are likely to be met with blank stares or defensiveness. (Weren't you defensive when your parents asked you these types of questions?)

Often your children simply don't have the right answer. They don't know what you need them to say to get them out of trouble. And most of us learn early on that we shouldn't raise our hands unless we have the right answer. In these situations it's important to be honest with what's really going on.

You can be feeling angry, frustrated, scared, or confused and allow your emotions to run the show. Perhaps you have no idea what you should do next to keep your child safe. Being present and open to your experience in the moment, and allowing yourself to really be seen by your child, allows them to open up to the same sort of vulnerability. Once you have cleared out your emotions, you might be able to ask questions that can invite real communication.

We don't advise starting this type of question asking in the middle of conflict. Learning to ask questions like this is a bit like learning how to drive a car when you are on a racetrack and the starting gun has just gone off. Creating connection with your children, asking them questions when there is not a crisis, shows your children that you really are interested in them and that they can come to you when they need to.

Begin by asking them questions about things that they are interested in. Ask questions of your partner and friends over dinner that offers the same level of respect. Particularly since our children are always changing, every conversation can be like meeting someone new. Giving them the space and expressing interest in who they are becoming, without being suffocating, can open a lifelong bond.

This is a helpful skill to use anywhere in your life. Asking questions allows people to reveal themselves to you. It gives us a chance to let go of many of the assumptions that we have about others and simply let them show up as they are.

Always ask questions - don't assume you understand someone especially when you have an emotional reaction. Take a breath and then ask, "Did you mean to...What I heard you say was...did I get that right?" Even if you heard right, they often might not have understood since they too were acting out of fear. Just hearing can clarify for them and change the dynamic. This can be particularly helpful for children and adolescents who are still learning their emotional vocabulary.

As I was working on this chapter, a client called me. He had been having some difficultly at work communicating with a manager. He really respects her and yet they often find they don't understand each other. We spent a session strategizing ways that he might step outside of himself to really hear what she was saying, to connect to the language she was speaking.

This was a big step since most our communication is actually focused on getting our point across and we miss what the other person is interested in communicating. Next time we spoke, he excitedly reported that he had used the tools I was teaching him and found that instead of having to repeat himself three or four times to be understood, his most recent communications had been smooth and easy. They weren't best friends but he felt like they had been able to work together at a higher level.

When we step outside ourselves and our own reactions for a moment to watch what's going on as if we were an observer watching a movie, we can be surprised by what we see. This is beginner's mind, the capacity to see something again for the first time.

Do you remember what it was like to drive a car for the first time? To kiss for the first time? To go on a job interview for the first time? In all of these cases, you weren't really sure what would happen.

Take a moment and ask yourself how many questions you ask yourself. For each question that you ask, you open a space to reveal yourself. If you don't ask questions of yourself, what stops you?

One of the most powerful ways that I work with clients is to ask them to pull apart their unconscious processes that make life work. We all have these. You don't have to figure out how to get up in the morning or decide everyday if you will really go to work in the morning. You don't have to figure out if and how you will feed your children dinner. Most of the things we do throughout the day don't really require conscious attention.

Since so much of what we do is unconscious, we can miss how many faulty strategies we are running on autopilot. So I simply ask clients questions designed to help them see what it is they are really doing. This awareness often brings lots of laughter even while it is opening up new avenues for future actions.

How many questions do you ask your children? When you ask, do you assume you know the answers or do you allow yourself to be surprised? If there is still so much to surprise you about yourself, how could you possibly not be surprised by your children?

There are a number of games on the market now that offer questions you can ask in your family. These are a great start for families that want to keep learning about each other. One family I know asks a question each time they gather for dinner and sees what everyone has to say. You can start this today by asking your family some of these: What are you happy about today? What did you learn today? Who did you really enjoy being with today? What did you notice for the first time or again after a long time today? When you ask questions never assume you know the answer. Leave yourself open for all the surprises that life is waiting to offer you!

Affirmation

Asking questions allows the people in our lives to reveal themselves. It also provides them with a way to be seen. Say the following ten times, "I joyfully ask questions that allow people to reveal themselves. I receive every answer, no matter the depth, with profound gratitude."

Self-Observation

How often do you ask questions? For the next few days, notice how many questions you ask where you genuinely listen to the answer. Record your observations in your journal.

Practice

No matter how many questions that you found you asked in your observation, practice asking more this week. Begin with your family and ask each person at least two questions a day that allow them to reveal a little more of themselves. It could be as simple as asking your children about a band they like or taking them to a movie they want to see and asking them a few questions after it.

Make sure that you include yourself as you ask questions. You might start with questions like:

- What am I really proud of lately?
- What's getting me excited?
- What is my heart really longing for?

Allow yourself to be surprised by the person who shows up.

Chapter 17: Live in the Fullness of Time

"We must not allow the clock to blind us to the fact that each moment in life is a miracle and a mystery."

~ H.G. Wells

"Time is too slow for those who wait, too swift for those who fear, too long for those who grieve, too short for those who rejoice, but for those who love, time is eternity."

~ Henry Van Dyke

Our world runs faster and faster every year. There always seems to be the tick tock of a clock in the background, a next appointment to get to, or a task to be accomplished. In the midst of this, many parents have established drive by relationships with their children and partners. They barely have time to talk to their friends and aren't even sure what they are really getting out of all this craziness.

Many have begun to realize that we are living in a time of great time sickness. Having lost our way, we are simply trying to fill up our time with more. Whether it's more things, more experiences or more people, as our scope expands our depth diminishes. The Canadian journalist, Carl Honore, saw this for himself when we was pondering buying a book of one-minute bedtime stories to read to his daughter at night.

How many minutes do you have for what's really important to you? How in control are you feeling of your time? Take a minute and ask yourself if you are doing too much in your day? How often in the last week have you needed caffeine to keep you awake? How often have you felt like you had more on your plate than you could possibly handle?

This evening, writing this chapter, an email arrived. A speaker that I plan to see tomorrow night wrote to tell us that she would not be able to attend the event. Her beloved husband had passed away.

Death is the ultimate test of time. In reality we only have so much time to live and yet we constantly waste it on work that is unimportant so that we can buy things that we don't want. But when the party's over, it doesn't really matter what you bought. The one with the most toys doesn't actually win.

More than anyone, children suffer from constant busyness. When your life is too full for you to bring your whole self into your relationships with your children and your family, how can you expect anything but partial relationships? But most of us have no idea where to even start to lessen our load and create more time in our lives. It might feel like asking you to do just one more thing might cause your head to explode. We suggest five strategies that can help you free up more time and energy in your life so that you can actually slow down.

Make a stop doing list.

There's an old saying that goes, "When you're in a hole, stop digging!" One of the easiest ways to free up time is to stop doing the things that aren't really serving you. Sometimes we get so attached to the way that we are living, to the habits that are ingrained in our lives, that we can't imagine living without them. And they often start completely by accident.

Not long ago, I realized that I was stopping my work each day at 1 to watch a television program while I was having lunch. I actually like the show but it had become a habit that I engaged anytime I was home. When I thought about it, I realized that I didn't really care if I watched this show, I had just turned it on for a break one day while having a bite and before I knew it, it was on everyday. When I decided to turn it off, I opened up a different experience of my lunch and ended up with about half an hour more time each day.

Anything that you are doing in your life that is not serving you can be released. You can make a choice right now. One of the best ways to figure this out is to do a time journal for a week. Just write down what you are doing throughout the day, hour by hour. Are you taking fifteen or twenty minutes to get a coffee when you could be taking a walk? Are you watching TV that you don't even really like? You can simply decide to stop doing anything that is not serving you allowing more time, space and expansion in your life.

Affirmation: "I freely release everything in my life that is not serving me and my greater purpose."

Be more mindful about what you say yes to.

It can be hard to say no. Saying no to people can activate a whole host of negative self talk along with fears about whether people will like us, what will happen if we fail to meet their expectations and whether we should do what they've asked.

But here's the kicker. Most of the time you know, even before you say yes, that you should say no. Your intuition speaks loud and clear with a queasy feeling in your stomach or hesitation. Learning to say no is one of the most liberating things that you can do for yourself.

William Ury has an excellent book called <u>The Power of a Positive No</u>. His simple concept of saying no to things that don't bring you life so that you can say yes to things that do has been life changing for many of our clients. When you are clear about your purpose it is easier to say no while affirming your own higher purpose.

Imagine that Suzie has just asked you to serve on the PTA Leadership Committee. It's an important position that you know would really help the school. But you also know that it will take you away from spending time with your children. You can say to Suzie, "Thank you so much for the invitation. I know how important this work is to the school. However, I am committed to spending more time with my family right now and will have to decline." It's hard for people to argue with our deepest commitments and if they do, it's much easier for us to stand resolved in our decision.

Affirmation: "I can say no to anything that doesn't fit into my life's purpose. By saying no to these things, I am saying yes to myself and to my life."

Complete or release unfinished business.

There are lots of things that can keep us feeling stressed and out of time especially when we remember that while time is static our experience of it is not. One of the great time zappers for us can be unfinished projects or business. They are like holes in a bucket and no matter how hard you try to fill the bucket, there is always a leak of your power or energy.

It's helpful to take a few hours and inventory all of the projects that feel unfinished in your life. These can be things around the house, relationships that never got closure or old papers you still want to file. It doesn't matter what they are, just that they are taking up real estate in your head and making your experience of time feel limited.

Once you have your inventory, ask yourself, on a scale of 0 to 10, how important are these tasks in relationship to your life purpose. Does it really matter whether your CD collection isn't alphabetized? Do the walls in the attic really need painting? Consider which of the old tasks that have been weighing on you for way too long can simply be released.

For any task that you can't release, pick at least one person that you can ask to help you complete it. If you need to get your backyard cleaned up so your children can play in it, ask friends or neighbors to come over and assist. You'd be amazed what a home cooked meal and a few beers can get done. You can also enlist your family to help. It's great if you can find a way to turn these tasks into games. Maybe the one who pulls the most weeds wins a prize. Finally, you can pay people to help you do tasks like extra filing or garage clean up. There are probably a number of local teenagers who could use some extra cash and wouldn't mind helping out. If you don't know anyone, check out craigslist, your local community service organizations or the yellow pages.

Affirmation: "I fully commit to completing or releasing any old business that is weighing me down. I am creating more life and lightness with each project I complete or release!"

Let go of some of the stuff in your life.

If you're like most people, you spend a lot of time taking care of things. Just about everything we own requires some degree of care and maintenance. Letting go of things that we no longer want or need can create lots more time in your life. And if you aren't using things, chances are someone else could really use them.

Matthew and Terces Englehart have a great phrase, "Relish it or release it." I have taken this phrase to heart and gone through everything in my home with a mindful eye. Not only does letting go of things that you are not using free up space in your home and time that you no longer have to care for those things, it also feels great giving things to people who need them or selling things to have more resources for what you'd really like to be doing.

Affirmation: "I am joyfully releasing anything in my life that I don't love or can't use."

Let go of the things that numb you so you have time for things that feed your soul.

There is a special category of things that don't serve us. These are the distractions that literally numb us to the world and usually distract us from what we are really seeking. Generally these are somehow entertaining. Inventory your life and ask yourself whether the amount of TV time, the dinners out, the $4 cups of coffee, the drinks after work, are truly entertaining you or just distracting you from your sense of purpose. Only you can be the judge of what's distracting you or serving you. But if something is taking away from your aliveness or is a guilty pleasure, you can choose to release it.

Affirmation: "I am freely releasing anything in my life that stands in the way of living my purpose."

Affirmation

When our lives feel too full, busy and out of control we often shortchange what is really important. Say the following affirmation ten times, "I have all the time I need to do what's truly important to me. I joyfully commit to releasing anything that steals time from my life's purpose!" Repeat it as needed.

Self-Observation

For a week, take notice of how you actually spend your time. We often don't have much awareness of how much time we are actually spending engaging different activities. Write this down noting how you are actually spending all of your waking time in the day. What patterns do you notice?

Practice

Based on your observations, you probably noticed at least one of the ways that you are using time unskillfully could be addressed using the five tools in this chapter. Pick any one of them and take it on as your practice. Feel free to do all five if you like but if you choose to do that, do only one at a time. Having one open project that you complete is much more satisfying and likely to get done than five that you have started but not finished.

Chapter 18: You Are Worthy

"You yourself, as much as anybody in the entire universe, deserve your love & affection."

~ Buddha

"At bottom every man knows well enough that he is a unique being, only once on this earth; and by no extraordinary chance will such a marvelously picturesque piece of diversity in unity as he is, ever be put together a second time."

~ Friedrich Wilhelm Nietzsche

No matter how successful they are, for many clients I see, they struggle with an underlying sense of unworthiness. They can't seem to believe that they are good enough to be loved, to have what they want in life or to achieve their higher purpose. So much of their work is releasing this old story of unworthiness since it creates expectations of how their lives should go.

As we have seen in earlier discussions, our expectations can be suffocating. They literally choke the life out of new possibility as they only allow life to show up in the way we have imagined. Our expectations are often rooted in evaluations of whether something is worthy or not. This includes the expectations that we place upon ourselves and our loved ones. And our evaluations of others' worthiness are usually a mirror of our own sense of worthiness.

We all grew up in a system that told us when we were worthy. In school, we got good grades and we advanced. We got bad grades and we stayed behind. When our parents were pleased with us, we got positive reinforcement and loving attention. When our parents were displeased, we got negative reinforcement and punishment. This sense of order is deeply ingrained in many of our religious traditions where we have to prove ourselves to be good enough to enter the Kingdom. In some religious traditions, there is some mark that we are never allowed to know that determines whether we gain admission or not.

And, we have to hope there isn't someone who is really, really worthy who throws off the curve and lands us back in the reject pile.

Trying to be worthy or deserving of love, attention, care or compassion is completely exhausting. No matter how long our list of reasons that we are "good" people, there are always other reasons why we are "bad." There are always ways that we have failed, are broken, and are unskillful. It's only when we give up this fight that we can know that these are false categories. By the nature of your humanity, you are a child of God. Your existence is your ticket to being worthy, loved and held by the universe.

Just as you are worthy by nature of your mere existence, so are your children, your spouse and your extended family. In fact, this includes everyone you have ever met. This means that no matter what your children say, do or think, they are always worthy of your love. This has not always been the case. There are far too many children that have been ejected from their homes because of their sexual orientation. There are others who lose family support and love because of the choices they make in terms of career, love or family. In my family, my grandmother was disowned by her father because she decided to marry an American soldier and move to the U.S. after World War II. Recently, a friend told me of a woman that she knows who has stopped talking to her daughter because she chose a partner who wasn't up to her standards.

Who does any of this rejection and evaluation serve? No one comes out a winner from this battlefield. In part, this is because any time we choose to reject another, to eject them from our hearts, we are ultimately rejecting a part of ourselves. If we had complete and unconditional love for ourselves, if we understood that our worth is not based on a score or is in any way up for question, then we would know that all people have this same level of worth. But when we reject others, it reinforces our own notion of how unworthy we really are.

There is a difference between releasing someone and rejecting them. I am not suggesting that you need to remain physically connected to a person to continue to love them and honor their worth as a human being. There are times when other people are damaging to us, put us in places of harm, or tear us down and the only answer is to separate from them. Releasing the hold that people who behave toxically have on us can be a form of self-care and love. However, if in the process we make them sub-human, less than or other, we damage ourselves while having very little impact on them.

Take a moment and reflect on the people that you are currently ejecting from your heart. What part of yourself are you choosing not to engage by doing this? Are there people that you might release from your life? What might that serve?

Let me give you an example of the difference. We all have known many couples in the course of our lives. Some break up and some stay together. Imagine for a moment, two young men who break up with their girlfriends. The first can only talk about what a bad person his lover was. He calls her names and spends his days complaining about the way that she damaged him.

In this scenario, he is projecting his judgment all over his ex-lover. Because she was unskillful in whatever way in the relationship, he believes she is no longer worthy of dignity. Since I've never seen a relationship that hasn't had two sometimes unskillful people, his notion that because she wasn't good in the relationship comes right back on himself. When he starts to pay attention, he will realize that he is responsible for some of the breakup. When this happens, his own worth is called into question.

A second young man, after a break up may simply understand that both parties were unskillful in some ways and their level of unskillfulness didn't work together. Neither he nor his ex-partner are bad people, and perhaps, if he is willing to look at his own role in the breakup, he might see how he is able to learn something from the experience.

Both men can create distance from the "ex" but for the first man, his ex-lover has been ejected from his heart. For the second, she has simply been released to find someone who she can be happy with. And since he has not poisoned the well of relationship, he is much more likely to be able find a better match for himself as well.

The beginning of accepting anyone into your life is to accept yourself, to understand that you are fundamentally worthy and that no action, good or bad, can shift that. When you know that you are worthy, you can allow your children to be worthy as well. Experiencing your worth is ultimately just a choice. If you try to prove it to yourself, you will always fail. You will be evaluating by the wrong standards. It is your birthright to be worthy as it the birthright of your children. We don't have to prove or do anything to get this. It is right here all along.

This is one of the most powerful teachings that you can pass on to your children. Knowing that we are worthy regardless or whether we succeed or fail opens us up to a whole new world of possibility. Imagine if your child believes that their worth comes from a grade they get on a test. If they want to test their own thinking and offer an answer that pushes the envelope, they will be limited by knowing that there is a judgment being passed on who they are based on the results. On the contrary, if they know they are worthy they can try something, fail and it doesn't threaten their core identity. When we know that all of life is learning, that we are worthy regardless of the outcomes, we can succeed or fail and still get right back up on the horse and keep riding!

Affirmation

We are all worthy by nature of our existence. Our birth is our ticket to all the gifts of the universe. Say ten times, "I joyfully acknowledge my unconditional worth. I freely receive all the gifts of the universe. Thank you! " Repeat this throughout the day when you find yourself judging yourself or other people.

Self-Observation

For a week, take notice of how often you judge other people as well as yourself. How often do you have to make them bad to feel good about yourself? How often do you make yourself feel smaller than you would like to be? Notice if there are any patterns and write them down in your journal.

Practice

The practice of radical acceptance can be difficult. We have been trained to think of things in categories of like or dislike, good or bad. For one week, practice seeing others through the eyes of their loving mother holding them as an infant at birth. See them as completely perfect and whole. Practice looking at yourself in the mirror seeing yourself like this as well as seeing others in this way. Notice how this shifts your relationships.

Chapter 19: Celebrate Your Mistakes

"Anyone who has never made a mistake has never tried anything new."
~ Albert Einstein

"There is no failure only feedback."

~ John Grinder and Richard Bandler

In our journey of life, we are all constantly learning. We are learning new skills, being introduced to new music, learning to be in relationship with other people and learning to follow our hearts as we pursue our higher purpose. In the midst of this, there is always messiness. How could any of us expect to be perfect in the process of learning? But this is exactly the expectation that we often place on ourselves and our children.

The education that many of us received was based on learning the right answer. We were expected to raise our hands when we knew the right answer in class. Much of our education has been geared around knowing an answer on a standardized test such as the SAT, or GRE, where memorization is rewarded and independent thought punished. There is little emphasis on the way that we get to the "right" answer or the notion that in life there are often many answers that work. Much less the basic truth that learning most often comes out of failure and messiness. It pushes us to try something new.

It's very easy to carry this mentality over into parenting. As we talked about in the last chapter, we often evaluate ourselves and others to determine whether they are worthy or not. Many parents hold up a mirror to the cracks and scars that show up in their children. The more we mirror that back, the more they identify with a sense of brokenness. For many of us, most of the attention we got as children came in the form of criticism. With overworked and overwhelmed parents, it's only natural that they would notice what we did wrong more than what we did right. The things that could put us in harm's way were often more important to notice to protect us than those things that would help us grow.

In his book, <u>The Success Principles</u>, Jack Canfield recounts the story of a little boy who decided he wanted a glass of milk. In attempting to get the bottle of milk out of the refrigerator it dropped to the ground making a milky mess of the kitchen floor. When his mother saw what had happened she laughed at the mess. "What a big mess! Would you like some help learning how to get the milk down?" They cleaned the mess up together and then went to the backyard where they experimented to find the best way for his small hands to bring down the jug.

What would happen if we all adopted that mother's approach to life? An approach that says that all of life is learning rather than making sure we are doing what's "right," staying out of trouble or keeping our heads down? What if we celebrated the stories of healing and the scars that went along with them as badges of honor in a life of learning? (The alternative to continually showing them negatively is to deny them pretending that nothing ever happened. But we know that whatever we resist persists so denial is no better a strategy.)

Noted psychologist Carol Dwek Ph.D., has done extensive research on the way we approach life. In her work, she identified two basic mindsets that most people learn as children and carry throughout their adult lives unless there is intervention. She calls these the growth and the fixed mindset. For those that live in the fixed mindset, life is really about being perfect, having people praise them, not rocking the boat. There is limited opportunity for learning because folks in this mindset don't want others to see them in places that are "messy." The alternative is a growth mindset that sees the world as a playground full of interactive experiences from which to learn and develop. Someone with the growth mindset probably came up with the Chinese proverb, "fall down seven times, get up eight." This way of seeing the world is based in much greater freedom. The corollary in what we've been discussing is abundance (growth) mentality and scarcity (fixed) mentality.

Whether we call it growth, optimism or abundance mindset, many studies concur that people who live with a growth mindset are happier, live longer, have more friends and are overall more successful in life. Perhaps this is because when obstacles arise, people with a basic growth mindset see opportunities. They can reframe difficulties into challenges to be met.

Obviously, no one lives entirely in one mindset or the other. It's a continuum where we all move forward and backwards to varying degrees. But we generally find a center point that we return to. Dwek, as well as quite a few cognitive behavioral psychologists, has been able to help most people who wants to move into a more growth-oriented mindset do so. It goes back to our first pathway. The shift begins by choosing the way that you are going to see an experience.

The beginning of living in a growth mindset is realizing that all life experiences open up the possibility of learning. No matter what events arise in our lives, we always can learn more about ourselves and open up to new possibilities. This shift is profound for many people and often can be greatly assisted by the support of a coach. It's no surprise that we often work with our clients to shift into new mindsets. It often takes a partner to help see and reflect back what's been invisible to support deep and lasting change.

Take a minute now to think about some recent challenges in your life. Maybe you have been having some financial difficulties or your boss has been difficult. Maybe you are having a particularly hard time communicating with your child. What might you be able to learn from this experience? What truths might open up for you?

Maybe you are okay doing this with minor challenges but perhaps you have a list of things that we believe there is nothing to learn from. They were just too hard or too horrible. When we have areas like this in our lives, experiences that were too painful to learn anything, it can wall off parts of our experience of ourselves. We may think these are small areas but imagine that your heart is a conduit, or a pipe, through which love and abundance flow in and out.

Even the smallest blocks such as resentments that you are carrying, anger you have with friends and family, things you haven't forgiven, can all restrict the flow of love through our lives. So if you have a bunch of small blockages plus a big block or two that is just too horrible to approach, imagine how much more clogged your piping is. If the universe is basically an abundant place where there is love waiting for you at every turn, can you see where keeping this kind of block would prevent you from experiencing much of what the world is trying to offer you?

Knowing that a growth mindset is one of the strongest predictors of lifelong happiness and success, wouldn't you prefer that your children enjoy a growth mindset? Wouldn't you prefer to live with a growth mindset yourself? Take a few moments now and think about recent challenges that you may have had with your children. Are there any times where they were just trying to learn? Could you have helped by making messiness in learning okay or assisting them in experimenting with how they might be able to succeed?

One of the most powerful ways that you can help your children see that all of life is learning is to be able to boldly admit your own mistakes. In our culture, it takes a degree of courage and humility to do this but without it, it is very hard to move forward in life. Parents particularly want to place themselves in a position of being all knowing. In part, this is because all parents truly want to believe that their actions will protect their children. To question your actions questions your ability to actually be that protector. At other times, life just seems too busy to have the conversations. Sharing times when you were mistaken and asking your children for help and brainstorming will set a powerful example that making mistakes is a tool of learning.

There is an old saying that goes, "Give someone a fish, feed them for a day. Teach them to fish, feed them for life." Giving answers to your children as to how they can solve their problems often doesn't serve them in the long run. It can teach them that their answers have to come from someone or somewhere else.

When your children are learning, you can be most helpful by creating a learning environment for them that is safe to fail. In the story of the mother and child with the milk jug, the mother took the milk jug filled with water to the backyard and helped her son think through how he might be able to get it down better. They experimented to see how his small hands could best retrieve the jug. The mother's hands weren't the same size and only her son could really come to the best answer. The learning came from experimentation and problem solving.

All of their lives your children will be learning. They will encounter new challenges whose solutions may not be obvious. In fact, with global warming and other challenges, the whole of humanity is in a situation where we don't have all the answers. What will best serve us is our capacity to learn in new situations, to experiment, to reason and to explore? The more that you are able to pass those skills onto your children, the more powerful lives they will be able to live!

Affirmation

We are all on a learning journey in life. Perhaps it's to learn to love, to hope, to trust or to be bold. It can be hard to see what we are learning in the midst of it. Say ten times, "I am joyfully embracing the lessons life is teaching me. I see every challenge as an opportunity to learn more."

Self-Observation

For the next week notice when you allow yourself to be oriented towards growth. Pay attention to how you perceive interruptions and unexpected events. Notice if there are any patterns and write them down in your journal.

Practice

We can always choose to live with a more growth-oriented mindset. At its core, it's really about reminding yourself that the obstacles in your life are opportunities to learn and exploring those opportunities.

On a piece of paper, draw three columns. In one column, make a list of the major obstacles in your life right now. In the second column, imagine what each of these things might be teaching you. What quality of being or truth could you learn from this? This one can be hard. Don't be afraid to ask your friends or just meditate for a bit and ask your intuition for guidance. Finally, in the third column write as many actions that you could do to embrace the challenge and lean into the learning rather than resisting it. Decide on one action to take this week for each of your challenges and follow through with it. Ask for help if you need it! Learning doesn't need to be a solitary adventure.

PART IV: POWER

Chapter 20: Being With What Is

"There are joys which long to be ours. God sends ten thousand truths, which come about us like birds seeking inlet; but we are shut up to them, and so they bring us nothing, but sit and sing awhile upon the roof, and then fly away."

~ Henry Ward Beecher

Today after an amazing lunch with some colleagues I decided the day was too beautiful to return immediately to the office. I had a few errands that I could run which would allow me to enjoy being outside. At one point, I stopped into a market to buy a mass transit pass. It's a bit of a strange process as they are only available at the customer service desk.

Today no one was at the desk. (This was the first time I've experienced this.) The woman in front of me was very anxious and I watched her frustration rise to the point of banging on the customer service window. I went over and asked a clerk to page for assistance. This didn't seem to calm her agitation. I could only imagine what story this woman was telling herself to get so upset about such as short wait. Finally, the clerk came, she was assisted and she hurumphed off much like Winnie the Pooh's friend Eeyore.

What I found fascinating was the choice she made in how she would use her energy in this situation. I was listening to my Ipod and enjoying the time. The man behind me didn't seem particularly concerned by the wait. And yet she was willing to burn up her energy in frustration.

Perhaps this is because we seem to love to complain. We tell people about our aches and pains. We rattle on about the people at work who drive us crazy. We talk about how our kids just never seem to listen even if we talk till we're blue in the face. And not only does very little change, it actually seems like things get worse. Why wouldn't they? We've been practicing how bad things are and practice makes plenty.

I'm sure the woman in line expected fast service and perhaps she had somewhere she needed to be. And I don't think these are unreasonable expectations. But I couldn't help but wonder if there were other choices available to her.

Occasionally, I notice this pattern when working with a new client. I feel like they are approaching life like an airplane pilot waiting for the right conditions to take off. They have filled the tanks; in fact, many are sitting on the runway and continue to fill 'er up even though the tanks are full. They are washing and waxing and waiting for life to show up in the right way for them to be happy, to live and to take off. And while they wait, the marvelous vehicle they have been given sits dormant, the world is going unexplored and they are unhappy because they don't have what they want. They are missing all the opportunities in front of them because they are unwilling to see life as it is. Instead, they see life only through the story of, "I can start when..." or "I will really be happy when..."

Unfortunately, life rarely shows up exactly as you imagine it. Can you imagine wishing that you could somehow have a bright red Ferrari for your whole life? You long to take it out onto the open road, feel the wind in your hair and its amazing power to turn tight corners on a dime. When a bright blue Ferrari shows up, you have gotten so attached to the earlier form that you can't accept it.

The nature of life is that the only time we actually have to live is in the present. The only time that you have to engage your power in the world is right now. And the best way to do that is to begin to see what's in front of you right now.

We have greater capacity to take purposeful action when we are open to seeing what's in front of us. And sometimes that action is purposeful waiting like when we know we are too upset to say what we really mean or we feel like we just want to lash out. It makes sense to wait a while before we talk to the person who has upset us.

When we talk about power, we make a clear distinction between power and force. Our culture is more familiar with forceful actions. When we yell at someone, make them feel small, strike them or attack them, we are using force. But we are also using force when we absorb the abuse of another, allow ourselves to be screamed at or disempowered.

Some of the characteristics of "forceful action" are:

- **Unidirectional** – Force only goes one way and is usually directed at someone or something.

- **Coercive** – The goal of force is usually to make someone different than they are.

- **Non-ecological** – Forceful actions don't generally consider the system that they are a part of. Essentially, if it's what I want, then it's good.

- **Win/Lose** - In order for me to win, you usually have to lose and vice versa.

- **Limits choices** – Since forceful actions rarely present the goal to the system, they are limited in their possibility to generate choice.

- **Damages relationships** – In the end, forceful actions usually create less space for authentic relationships to flourish.

There are times when forceful actions are appropriate. If your child is about to run into traffic, yelling and grabbing them is the most appropriate thing to do. You are responding to immediate need. But often once the danger has passed, parents can continue to act forcefully even when powerful actions would be more useful in helping children learn.

The characteristics of powerful actions are:

- **Multidirectional** - Powerful actions usually begin at a deeper level grounded in values more than desires. These actions engage the whole system in creating change.

- **Adaptive** – Realizes the most powerful way to shift a system is to shift ourselves first.

- **Share power** – Since the goal is more systemic change, they tend to share power with all the parties involved enlisting their help in creating change.

- **Ecological** – They consider the consequences of the action on the whole system. How does this affect other people and the planet?

- **Win/ Win** – Powerful actions aim to find a way that

everyone's highest intention can be met. This usually creates more creative solutions and longer term compliance.

- **Expands choices** – Since powerful actions can engage multiple people or perspectives, they tend to expand the choices that are seen and are available.

- **Builds relationships** – While you can't make everyone happy all the time, including people in the process allows them to feel better about actions even when they aren't the ones they would have chosen.

Our goal in working with clients is to expand the array of choices that are available in any given situation. Being able to choose actions that align with your true intentions enables a more expansive, free life. In this way, **power is the capacity to choose any of the options before you or to create new ones in a way that brings the greatest wellbeing to a situation.** This requires that you be present enough to see the choices and that you have enough tools in your tool belt to respond in more than one way. You've heard the old expression, "If all you have is a hammer then everything looks like a nail." You have to see what's really in front of you to be able to pick the right tool to address the situation.

The beginning of all power, like abundance, is simply to be with what is - to receive life for the gift that is presenting itself to you right now. In fact, the greatest power that you can ever have is to simply accept what is in front of you. You might ask, "Do you mean I'm supposed to accept my boss who's treating me badly or my lover who is cheating?" We're not suggesting that you should or shouldn't do anything in particular (there is no imperative in our perspective) but simply that you have the capacity to choose just to let it be, to not expect it to be something different than what it is and then be angry with it for not meeting your expectations.

You give away your power when you decide that something MUST change. First, understand that whether you decide it must change or not, it is changing. The nature of life is change. The people in the situation are getting older, their bodies are changing, their thoughts are changing, the world is turning and the seasons are changing.

Second, desire to change a situation often comes out of anxiety about letting a situation run its course. When we are uncomfortable we have been taught that we should do something to fix it now. The whole of our culture teaches us this with incessant advertising that we should run right out and see a movie or buy a treat to calm us down whenever we are feeling a little anxious. If you react to your anxiety, you have a much narrower range of options from which to choose. You are seeing out of a small lens that focuses on your need to quell your anxiety and may miss out on the larger dynamics of what's going on. What are the needs of the other people that aren't getting met? What is really going on here? What question could I ask that could open up dialogue and shift the situation?

In our families, we are often waiting for people to show up in a different way until we choose to really connect with them. As long as they don't, we keep a safe distance or leave the dynamic just as it is. This often happens in cases where people are addicted to a substance. Family members will choose not to interact with them unless they are in recovery. Or for others, they will not respond to a request from their children unless it's asked for in a certain way. There is no thought to what the real need is underneath the request. Imagine if to get anything in your life you had to fill out forms like at the DMV, exactly right, and if you didn't you were sent back into the line to start over. Sometimes parents act like DMV agents with their children seeing their needs only when they are presented in a certain way.

Just as life rarely shows up as we might hope (often it shows up in far more exciting ways than we planned), our families show up in ways that are unexpected. Children can be "difficult". They can be unskillful and you might not know how to support them. But you have this one life to really see what's in front of you and act.

Opening up to acting in power allows you to choose actions in alignment with who you are. It also gives you the ability to empower others as you build deeper relationships.

Affirmation

When we are able to be open to what's in front of us, without wishing that it was somehow something else, we have much greater capacity to act. Say ten times, "I am open to life exactly as it shows up. All of life is a gift. Thank you!" Repeat this throughout the day.

Self-Observation

For the next week, watch where you are trying to exercise force in your life through controlling actions. Notice where you are waiting for life to show up in a particular way (a passive form of control) until you will act. Write these down in your journal and see if you notice any patterns.

Practice

Pick somewhere that you are very familiar with and choose to look at it in a whole new way. Like one of those picture finds where you look for what's hidden in an unexpected place. In this practice, simply look for things that you haven't noticed before. Make a list of 25 things (really, 25) that you haven't paid attention to before. One of the easiest ways to do this is to simply take in information from all of your senses. We rely primarily on our sight so now notice how this place smells, what textures are present, what sounds are in the background. See how your experience changes with this location knowing so much more about it. Realize this exercise is possible with the people and events in your life as well!

Chapter 21: Practice Ease

"All the fish needs to do is get lost in the water. All man needs to do is get lost in the Tao."

~ Chuang Tzu

There is an often-told story of a man who was stuck in a flood. He prayed and asked God to save him knowing that his faith would prevail. Early in the day, his friends offered him a ride to a nearby safe city.

"No thanks. God will save me," he told them as they drove out of town.

The rain continued to fall and soon was well over ten feet high. As he stood on the second floor of his house looking out his window, his neighbors pulled up in a boat and offered him a ride.

"No thanks, God will save me," he said confidently.

And still the waters kept rising and the man moved to the roof. Soon a helicopter flew by, lowered the ladder and tried to convince the man to come along.

"No thanks, God will save me."

Finally, running out of gas, the helicopter left, the waters rose and the man drowned. When he got to heaven he asked God, "What happened? Why didn't you save me?"

God replied, "I sent a car, a boat and a helicopter. What more do you want?"

We can make life way too difficult for ourselves. The universe is hard at work supplying all our needs but they don't always show up the way we expect so we send them on their way and wait. We wait until the help we receive comes in just the form we want. We wait for people to love us just the way we want. It's like requesting information and restricting ourselves to hearing about it from what we receive in the mail.

While we wait we keep on telling ourselves our favorite stories. Just as we have stories about parenting, we also have stories about the way that universe works that make life much harder than it needs to be. They usually go something like this:

- It's us against them.

- I have to do it all for myself. No one else is going to help me.

- I'm alone in the universe.

- Life is hard.

- I have to look out for number one.

- No one really cares about me.

At the base of all these stories is a sense of extreme isolation and separation. This is the work of the ego, the part of the mind that spends its whole existence struggling. It's also the part that tells you that you shouldn't trust others because the world is an unsafe place. It is the part that believes the only way of affecting a situation is to control it.

This is definitely one story that we can tell about the world we live in. And clearly there is some truth in it. The world can be an unsafe place. We can live in spaces of isolation and loneliness. Not every one is worthy of blind trust. But isn't it possible there is something more to this story? Might we only be looking at the shadows and missing out on the light?

Most of the world's spiritual traditions tell stories of a basic intelligence of the universe, a leaning into life. Judeo-Christian traditions talk of the spirit or breath of God animating all of existence. Eastern traditions reflect a deep reverence for the way in which the natural world reflects an order and intelligence worthy of respect. Even scientists talk about basic principles of order in the universe that are oriented towards life.

The natural world, for the most part, lives in relative harmony. There is no waste and all action supports the continued existence of the living system. Even death promotes life for others in the natural world. Without someone to orchestrate it, make it more efficient or productive, the natural world functions better than any human has ever been able to imagine. There is a sense of ease in this.

This ease is also available to human beings. The simplest place to witness this ease is in our breathing. Take a moment, just one is enough, right now, and observe your breath. Watch as you inhale and exhale, as your lungs expand and contract, knowing that with each inhale you are taking in energy and with each exhale you are releasing energy. It is really quite marvelous in its simplicity while it generates the very force of our life.

If we didn't breathe, we would not live very long. It is one of the fundamental requirements for our lives and yet we give it no thought whatsoever. The fact that you have to pay attention to your breath to even notice the miracle that your body is performing many, many times each minute proves that.

In the West we have even been taught to breathe in an unnatural way. One of the first things a singer learns is how to breathe in alignment with the body, from the diaphragm rather than the chest so that we fill our whole body with life-giving oxygen. This simple shift creates a greater sense of calm and fills our bodies with more energy. The chest breathing that most of us do actually restricts the flow of oxygen. We are literally starving ourselves.

Laurence Boldt writes, in The Tao of Abundance, "We are so afraid to breathe - to really let the universe in and ourselves out. To do so, we must give up control. We must stop breathing and let the universe breathe through us. We must trust things as they are...We must stop doing and let the universe do us."

In Taoism, the universe is thought of like a river that is flowing along in one direction. Because the Taoists were such close observers of nature, they believed the direction that this river points is in the direction of life. All of nature is set up to support life. Animals and plants have an instinctual intelligence that tells them this is so. Humans, however, are capable of great freedom in our choices. We are free to choose if we want to swim with the river or against it or if we just want to float. Those that swim with the river are naturally going to get much farther than anyone else. But even those that float will travel farther than those that are swimming against the current. When you feel like you are working so hard and yet you are not getting the results that you want, ask yourself whether you are working with life or trying to control it? Are you pushing your agenda or are you being open to letting everything work in concert to achieve mutual satisfaction and harmony?

This basic concept of ease is called "wei wu wei" or effortless effort. It doesn't mean that you don't do anything in your pursuit of life but that you lean in the direction of life when you do it. Regardless of your philosophical background, you can probably remember times in your life when this has been true. When you worked too hard and choked the life out of something. If you are straining to make something happen, you are probably working too hard.

This is definitely true in our families. Think about when you try to force your children to talk with you, to be open and to share their feelings. They most often respond to the force because the deep intention, beyond what you are presenting, is your desire to control them. You have an idea of what their openness should look like and you are trying to force and strain to make it happen. However, if you can simply create space in yourself and in your family for expressions of caring and love to be practiced on a daily basis, there is a greater allowance for your children to reveal themselves to you in a way that works for them.

Take a moment now and think about any situations in your life where you are really struggling. Particularly if you have heard yourself say something to the effect of "no matter what I try, nothing seems to work." See if you can see how you might be trying to force this situation, to control its outcome rather than allow it to simply follow its own course. How might you shift your behavior to create some more space for this to happen?

Part of our resistance to leaning into life is our intense reliance on intellect. We use the mind to try to figure things out, control outcomes and change what is around us. But the part of our mind that we use is the linear part that only sees some of the picture. The part that believes that A causes B which results in C. This is a very simple view of the universe that limits the possibilities of life. Throw a pebble into any pond and you will see that its effect ripples out all across the waters. Our actions have consequences far beyond what our conscious minds are able to focus on.

We do have another part of our mind that is able to see a much wider span. Sometimes we call it the emotional brain or the right brain, other times we call it intuition or that small, still voice that speaks to us when we are truly open to listening. This part of ourselves that speaks with the head, the heart and the body can be a wise guide when we let it. It allows us to relax into actions that make deeper sense.

Test this out for yourself. Have you ever made a decision against the deep feeling in your gut that told you not to? How did it turn out? Have you ever made a decision that seemed totally illogical based on your deep intuition, that gut pull, even when you couldn't fully explain why? How did that work?

For most of us, when we are willing to work with our intuition, it provides insights that we are unable to access with our conscious mind. This intuitive sense can be particularly strong for mothers. Sometimes they seem to know when something's wrong with their children from the smallest, unfathomable clues.

If you want to move with ease, trust intuitive guidance. Simply breathe deeply a few times, let yourself touch deeply into the core of yourself and ask for a direction or answer to your conundrum. Some people practice this as prayer. Then simply release it and trust that you will know the answer when you see it.

With your children, you can move with the greatest ease when you allow yourself not to fight the process of them growing up. When you are able to be a guide or a coach, slowly giving them more and more control, and yet still being prepared to catch them when they fall. In doing this, you are teaching your children that true love doesn't seek to control but rather to empower. And there are few better lessons we can imagine in life!

Affirmation

Much of our learning in life can be how to work with life rather than to strain against it. Repeat this ten times, "I trust that that I am held by the universe. I am choosing to lean into life. I will allow my intuition to guide me."

Self-Observation

For the next week notice when you feel like you are putting in a lot of effort and not getting the results you want. Are there ways that you could release your grip, as if you were holding this person or event in your hand, as precious as a tiny bird, allowing it to take its time and stretch its wings when it's ready? Write down your observations in your journal.

Practice

Intuition is one of the strongest allies that we have in allowing ourselves to live a life of greater ease. Pick a situation this week that you have been particularly struggling with. What is it that you would like to know in order to move this situation into ease? Formulate a specific question like, "Should I trust him?" or "Is this job offer the right one for me?" If you have no idea, you can simply state your question, "What do I really need to know to make this decision?" Take a few deep breaths, touch deep into yourself and ask this question. Then just sit back and relax knowing that an answer will come to this question and you will know it when you see it.

Chapter 22: Invite Support

"We don't accomplish anything in this world alone ... and whatever happens is the result of the whole tapestry of one's life and all the weavings of individual threads from one to another that creates something."

~ Sandra Day O'Connor

"If you were all alone in the universe with no one to talk to, no one with which to share the beauty of the stars, to laugh with, to touch, what would be your purpose in life? It is other life, it is love, which gives your life meaning. This is harmony. We must discover the joy of each other, the joy of challenge, the joy of growth."

~ Mitsugi Saotome

"Asking is the beginning of receiving. Make sure you don't go to the ocean with a teaspoon. At least take a bucket so the kids won't laugh at you."

~Jim Rohn

We live on a planet with six billion other people. That's a number so big as to be beyond my comprehension. And yet, in the middle of this sea of people, we have become more and more isolated. We have disconnected and told ourselves that we have to do it all alone. We often spend our nights in front of the TV alone, eat alone and even when we are with others, we can feel that we can't really share who we are. We can spend our lives in crowded cities but we don't really need to connect to others to survive.

For most people I work with, this myth is one of the greatest obstacles to their success. They think that they have to do it all on their own. Not that they don't bring other people into the mix but it's often just to complain or vent. Because we have been so deeply convinced that we are all alone, we can't see all the ways that the universe offers to support us throughout our lives.

There is no doubt that the universe works to support life in all its forms. There is no form of life that I can find where the planet does not naturally provide for all its needs. There is a habitat and food and water for each creature as long as it is not polluted or destroyed by another species. Even humans have all of our basic needs provided by the planet. Our fuel, our food, our shelter, our clothing, these are all gifts from a planet that is working so hard to support us and yet we can't see it.

Take a moment just to let this basic truth sink in. Everyday that you have been alive has been thanks to the Earth, the Sun and the Moon. Not one day of your life has the sun decided to stop shining or the moon to keep the tides in line. Not one bite of food you have ever eaten has come from anything that the Earth did not provide the basic building blocks for. Not one molecule in your body is not thanks to this amazing universe that has recycled the bones of dinosaurs and bits of stardust to create you. Your existence is thanks to a universe that supports you every day. Can you breathe that in? Can you allow this simple truth into your heart?

If you're like me, you're tired of this lonely distortion that we have been assigning to the universe. You might want to celebrate this amazing planet and find a way to live that allows for the deep connection that so many of us are longing for. The place to begin is to ask for help, to offer your hand to others and to build community. We are a communal species and this is our very nature. I am amazed how often we expect other people to guess what we need and then are angry with them for not providing it. In part, I believe this is because we don't take the time to figure out what we really need.

Take a moment to think about a place in your life where you are struggling as well a place in your life where you are succeeding wildly. In both of these instances, imagine what you could ask others for to help you. In cases of struggle, ask how sharing this struggle could help you to allow it to pass or help you to learn the lesson available to you (maybe it's how to ask for help)? In cases of success, ask yourself what more you could accomplish if you allowed other people to assist you with this project? What new heights could you rise to? And what might be stopping you from doing just that? How much more amazing could your family be if you shared your hopes and dreams for your family, asked to hear theirs and then worked together to create that dream?

Asking for what we need can be one of the most powerful tools in our tool belt. It requires that we be able to check into ourselves to see what our real needs are and then being to able to articulate them.

In my work, I end up working with two kinds of needs. There are basic survival needs. These include housing, food, clothing and other things that your body relies on just to be able to function. Then there are the emotional/spiritual needs that we discussed earlier. These are the needs to be seen, to belong, and to create.

We often try to meet our deeper emotional needs with survival mechanisms. For example, have you ever been sad so you had too many drinks? We are trying to meet our need for another to connect with us deeply, to share our pain and to support us with alcohol. Or have you ever been bored so you turn on the TV? Perhaps you are feeling stifled in your capacity to create or your need for belonging so you try to distract yourself with entertainment. This is nowhere more obvious than in our relationship with food. We probably all have some sort of "comfort" food that makes us happy when we are feeling down or stressed. Ever eaten something to take away the sting of painful emotions?

Many, including psychologist Laurel Mellin, who has worked extensively with people living with addictions, have found that once emotional needs are met, cravings for everything from too much food to cigarettes to alcohol have basically disappeared. The need has been met. I use many of the awareness and basic meditation practices that you have been introduced to throughout this book for exactly this purpose. And the results can be dramatic. In part, because you can stop doing what's not working. When you realize that another glass of wine or piece of cake isn't really going to create the feeling you want and you can start to figure out what might, you are able to be truly liberated.

The beginning of this is simple awareness and waking up. When we meditate or practice awareness of our emotions, we become more capable of answering the question, "How are you?" We may be able to identify that in this moment we are feeling sad or happy or angry or silly or frustrated. We also will notice that our emotions arise and pass pretty quickly. We can move from happy to angry to sad in a moment.

Take two minutes right now and practice this basic emotional awareness exercise. Simply close your eyes and watch your breath. Each time an emotion arises, simply name it and allow it to pass. The purpose isn't to follow the emotion but rather just to notice that it arises. When you are done, what did you notice?

When I first teach this exercise to clients they are often amazed that they see as much as they did. It's fun to watch them in their first awareness practices notice boredom, frustration, anger, silliness. (They actually say them out loud with me.) And then to see them realize that all of those emotions exist within a very short span of time. It is only when we follow these emotions that they really take a hold of us. When we connect stories to them and attach to them they can suffocate us.

Take one more moment, check in with yourself and notice how you are feeling. Are you feeling like your needs to be seen, to belong and to create are being met? If not, who could you ask for help?

The more we connect to others, discuss our needs, our hopes, our dreams together, the more we are able to build community. Our communities are the places where we can start to organize together to meet our needs. Our homes are the beginning of community. For thousands of years people lived in small, extended tribes that helped each other grow food, hunt, tell stories and initiate each other into adulthood. Only recently have we lost many of these traditional groupings.

In their place, people have turned to churches, self-help groups, nonprofit organizations and chosen families (communities that they have constructed for themselves.) All of these can be viable options for parents. Everyone needs help sometimes and having a support system to rely on can open up incredible possibilities. Realizing that no one can do it alone, many parents trade off weekends when the other watches the kids so they can have a weekend getaway. Or they share responsibilities such as carpooling, planning parties or preparing food. In what ways are you connected to a community where you can reach out for support? What communities exist for you in your area? If you have a child with special needs or special gifts, have you considered reaching out to parents on the Internet or groups in your area?

Finding or creating community takes a bit of work at the beginning. It means introducing yourself to new people, making small talk and allowing yourself to be vulnerable. It requires us to reach out to others and practice connecting in a world that is rapidly forgetting how to do this. But in the end, there is no substitute for having a group of people that you can rely on to help raise your children and yourselves. It really does take a village!

When children are raised by many people that love them, care for them, and listen to them, they know that they are loved. They learn how to connect with others. And they learn by watching their parents ask for help how to do so themselves. They learn to create wider connections and deeper relationships. And they learn that there is an alternative to the lonely world that so many people live in today. They learn to trust their hearts and open themselves to a world that is full of love and laughter if they are willing to reach out for it!

Affirmation

When we are supported in community, we are able to accomplish more than we can ever do alone. Repeat the following affirmation ten times now and as you like later. "I am held by the loving support of the universe (God, Allah, Buddha, my community...). I am allowing myself to receive support and connection in healthy, loving ways!"

Self-Observation

Notice for the next few days where you are telling yourself that you have to do it all alone, that there is no support, that it is you against the world. These may come in subtle ways or they may be quite obvious. Notice these places and write them down in your journal.

Practice

One of the most insightful, compassionate coaches I know, Michael Dolan, taught me this beautiful exercise to open our hearts, to allow ourselves to feel supported and to ask for what we need. With a friend or partner, someone that you feel very comfortable with, practice being held for ten minutes. In that ten minutes, if you would like the other person to make adjustments, simply request them. "Could you hold me tighter? Could you put your hand on my heart? Could you...?" The specific instructions aren't important but rather that you are asking for exactly what you need and allowing yourself to receive it. During the whole exercise keep checking back into your breath and your heart. Let yourself fully experience being held. Afterwards, write about how this felt in your journal.

Chapter 23: Stretch Your Boundaries

"Our firmest convictions are apt to be the most suspect, they mark our limitations and our bounds."

~ *Jose Ortega y Gasset*

The first time I got on a bike was pretty scary. I was about six years old and was graduating from my big wheel tricycle into the world of two wheels. My grandfather supported the bike as he ran along side me going back and forth down the street in front of their house. My mind was filled with pedals, brakes, balance and steering. There was so much to remember that I wasn't even sure that I wanted to do it even as I knew I wanted to learn more than anything.

Those first few rides were wobbly and a bit frightening. It seemed like a long way to fall. But soon I was sailing around the neighborhood behind my grandfather's bike and wondering when I would graduate to an adult-sized bike like the one he rode. I learned to ride faster and farther and later, my bike would become a source of independence as I rode around town on my own.

If you have read this far, chances are you have probably stretched your boundaries a bit. You might have been introduced to some new ideas and tried out some new practices. Take a minute to acknowledge and to congratulate yourself on your voyage outside of your comfort zone. It's only when we travel into this realm that we are able to really learn.

Leaving our comfort zone is not something we like to do much these days. We long to be comfortable in our world. The movie Wall-E has a great depiction of this where, in the world of the future, humans ride around in flying wheelchairs all day never even having to lift their arms to put their lattes to their mouths.

We often use our discomfort to disconnect from people and situations. "I just don't feel comfortable with that," is a phrase that ends many interactions. But life is not comfortable. It's bumpy and messy and emotional. Expecting life to be comfortable seems to be the mark of insanity to me.

So one of the most valuable things that you can do in your parenting (as well as your life journey) is to let go of the notion that anything should be comfortable. In fact, the first Noble Truth of the Buddha is that all life contains suffering (discomfort). Can you imagine if you were unwilling to experience the discomfort of growing? Your body would never expand, reach for the sky and move freely. Or if you were never willing to face the discomfort and possible embarrassment of a first kiss and all that has the potential to lead to? Our greatest moments of learning come from the places where we are forced, sometimes kicking and screaming, to stretch ourselves.

Parents are faced with this everyday. The older your children get, the less you are able to protect them. You are forced to rely on their good sense and strong values to guide them as they make choices about relationships, substance use, sex, jobs and all the important choices life presents them with. In a world where we control very little, it helps to make friends with this discomfort.

For many of my clients, discomfort brings anxiety. Right now we are experiencing a period of great discomfort as a culture. Our values are shifting, along with our priorities, as a new president has taken office and the economic situation requires significant change. In these periods of anxiety we get to make a powerful choice. We can choose to be present to discomfort, expand along with it, and learn in the process. Or we can deny the changes that we are living through. We can simply stick our heads in the sand and hope that everything will be back to normal when we decide to join the world again.

This kind of ostrich thinking is a common tactic for many people. But it gives up all our power to be part of the solution, to engage the world and create change. When clients choose to let go of this type of thinking and reframe the experience as one of possibility, they often see a whole new world opening up before them. For parents, this means that as your relationship is continually changing with your children, at each level you get the opportunity to be in relationship to a more deeply awake human being who has lots to teach you even as you guide and protect them.

The other option is to pretend that they are not growing older. You can continue to relate to them as if they were very small and new to the world acting as if your relationship to them is the same. Of course, your children are changing and won't respond in the same ways as they used to.

Can you imagine trying to do this in the natural world? Would you treat a seed the same as a seedling, or a mature plant the same as one that is dying? All through the cycle of life, we are changing and so are our relationships. Adapting and making peace with the discomfort of change can allow you to have a relationship with your children based on who they are rather than who they were.

Take a moment and imagine your children through the stages of growth that they have experienced up until this point. Imagine how you parented when they were a newborn? A toddler? Starting elementary school? An early adolescent? Later teen? Young adult? You already know that you are always changing just as all relationships are. The more you make peace with this, the more you will be able to be present to all the possibilities that this moment holds for your relationship with your children.

And you will be able to teach your children to move through pain and discomfort with more ease than you may have learned as a child. If you teach your children that the best things in life often come with some sort of messiness and discomfort, you instill in them a sense of perseverance and a will to continue even when the going gets tough. Winston Churchill, the Prime Minister of England during World War II, once said, "If you are going through hell, keep going!" What a great lesson to be able to teach your children!

To be sure, discomfort will show up in our lives. But the greater discomfort comes from the delusion that life should be comfortable. In teaching your children that sometimes our life's purpose requires that we give up some pleasure for a greater reward, you teach them the emotional intelligence skills that will serve them their whole life through.

Daniel Goleman, Ph.D., has been researching what makes people truly successful for decades. He conducted one long-term study of children in the early 80s. The test was simple. Children were left in a room with a marshmellow on the table in front of them. They were told that they could have that marsh mellow now or if they waited for ten minutes until the researcher got back they could have two. Many ate the first marshmellow while others waited. The fascinating part of the story is that twenty years later when they went back to see how their lives had gone, the children who were able to delay their gratification for ten minutes had done better in school, had better jobs and seemed to have greater levels of overall life satisfaction. A little bit of discomfort brought them greater pleasure and joy in the end and those skills had been serving them ever since!

There isn't much reason to like discomfort but when we live our lives avoiding it, we miss out on many opportunities for learning. Clients often tell me that they don't do something that will help their business because they don't like it. They don't like giving presentations or they don't like meeting new people. Or they don't really like writing. Most of the time, this boils down to the fact that they are uncomfortable with the skill because they have not given themselves the time to actually learn it.

The wobbling feeling, the lack of control, the uncertainty that we feel when we first are learning to ride a bike are things that no one really likes, but if we do not allow ourselves to experience them, we will never have the experience of riding on our own. If we do not practice a language or a musical instrument we will never move into mastery where it is a joy to play or speak with another.

This can be true of parenting skills as well. Parents sometimes don't want to talk with their kids about sex or drugs because they are uncomfortable. Parents may not like to discipline (create boundaries and consequences) for their children because it makes them feel bad. You may not like checking in with your own emotions or meditating because you touch into a lonely part of yourself that you would rather not admit is there. In all of these cases, if you are able to move past the discomfort into a level of mastery, your parenting skills greatly expand and you are able to have a deeper relationship with your children and yourself.

Discomfort will likely never be fun for anyone. But if you can keep coming back to the way that it is moving you toward your larger life purpose, it becomes much more manageable and in the end, you will have mastery over skills that you would never have had otherwise. What a lesson to teach your children to lighten their load in life!

Affirmation

Discomfort is a temporary state that passes if we allow ourselves to simply experience it. We get stuck in it when we believe we should never experience discomfort. Say to yourself ten times now and as often as you like later, "I am allowing myself to move through any discomfort that arises in my life with ease. I know that there is something to be learned in the challenges to life! Thank you!"

Self-Observation

For the next week, notice where you feel uncomfortable. What happens when you allow yourself to experience this a bit? Are you able to stay with the discomfort? Does it pass once you allow yourself to experience it? Record what you noticed in your journal.

Practice

Go back to any practice that you've skipped over because you thought you wouldn't like it. Realize that you don't have to like it but that you can use it as a way to let go of your discomfort. For one week, engage the practice trusting that you can survive the discomfort and you can let go of the desire to feel comfortable!

Chapter 24: Practicing Forgiveness

"To forgive is to set a prisoner free and discover that the prisoner was you."

~ Lewis B. Smedes

"Always forgive your enemies - nothing annoys them so much."

~ Oscar Wilde

If you were sitting in one of our workshops right now and we were talking about forgiveness, I might ask for a show of hands. Raise your hand if you ever had a fight with your child that left you really hurt. Raise your hand if you had a fight with your partner in the last year that you haven't fully let go of. Raise your hand if you have any anger over the way that your parents raised you. Raise your hand if you have done anything to your children that has made you feel like a bad parent. Before long, everyone's hand is up. It seems like we have a lot to forgive in our lives.

No matter what the wound, forgiveness is an act of kindness we do for ourselves. It does not mean that we forget it and place ourselves in an unsafe situation. Nor does it mean that we pretend it never happened or that it was okay. It means that we allow ourselves to fully experience the emotions of hurt, anger, betrayal and sadness that went along with the action and we release the bond of negativity that has been holding us down.

Many people believe that they must wait for the person who they wronged them to ask for forgiveness before they are able to give it. But since we understand that forgiveness is really a selfish act (in the best sense of the word), it doesn't matter if that person asks for it or not or even if they are still living.

Fred Luskin, author of <u>Forgive for Good</u> and Director of the Forgiveness Project at Stanford University, offers a powerful process for releasing pain and entering into forgiveness. I had the good fortune to learn much of this from him in person and was impressed by his graciousness. In the six-week course I took with him, I had no idea until half way through that his daughter had been killed in a car accident only six months before. He could have been raging at the world, God, himself or her, in his loss. He is clearly a man who practices what he preaches.

The basic steps of forgiveness

Feel the fullness of the hurt

Sometimes we prevent ourselves from really feeling the pain of an experience by attaching to the wrongness of it. Have you ever had a situation occur in which someone acted in a way that just seemed unbelievable? Perhaps you understood the circumstances in a totally different way and their actions were completely incongruent with that understanding. If you've ever been in a relationship where you thought the other person was really into you and then they abruptly broke up leaving you feeling completely in left field, you know what I mean. Or if you've ever felt like someone you really trusted betrayed your confidence, you've also probably experienced this.

And sometimes, even when we expect something is going to happen, we still hold onto the wrongness of it. A friend recently was given 60 days notice to move out of his apartment. The landlord had decided to sell the building. His initial response was one of disbelief and wondering if he had any recourse under the tenancy laws of the city. He wasn't allowing himself to really feel his frustration and grief over losing an apartment he really enjoyed living in.

Usually we vent to other people when we are in this situation. We tell them all the bad things the other person did and how we were wronged. Venting is really the wrong word for this type of experience because when we do it we aren't really releasing anything. Perhaps we should call it stoking (like stoking a fire) because it simply reinforces the story of wrongness without giving space for the emotions underneath it to be expressed and released.

So the beginning of the process of forgiveness is to really experience the emotions. The easiest way to do this is to share your hurt with one or two people that you trust. You don't need them to tell you how wrong it was or what they would have done in your place or even what you should do. You don't need them to fix it. Just ask them to allow you to share how you are feeling and really hear you.

We can't move beyond what we don't really allow ourselves to experience. One of the ways that we deny the pain of an experience is by blaming the other person or telling a story about how everything happens to us. No matter what the mechanism, in order to really forgive fully, we have to let the emotions move through us.

Realize and release your grievance story

Have you ever heard the story of the Emperor's New Clothes? The Emperor goes parading around the city completely naked after being convinced that he is wearing a beautiful, magical new set of clothes. No one in the town is willing to say anything for fear of embarrassing or upsetting the Emperor until one small boy speaks up and cries out, "The Emperor is naked!" With this declaration the spell is broken and everyone can acknowledge the illusion they've been participating in.

I wonder if part of you knows that the stories you tell about other people, about the ways that they hurt and wronged you, are only stories even as another part clings to them? We often like to tell the story of how people have done things to us. Perhaps in a sociopathic world this might be true. People might be running around solely with the intention of hurting other people.

Check in with yourself and see if, when you have done things that have hurt other people, your intention was first and foremost to damage them. For the most part, when we do things that harm other people, we are really trying to meet our own needs or sometimes we are acting in what we think is their best interest. This can often happen when we are concerned about someone.

The best testimony to the fact that our actions weren't about someone else but rather about meeting our own needs is how often we are surprised when we have hurt someone. Has that ever happened to you? You had no idea that what you were doing was irritating or upsetting another person but somehow you had been doing something that made them crazy? Or maybe they've interpreted your actions in a way totally incongruent with the way you understand what you've been doing?

There may even have been times when you were so angry that you did something for the purpose of revenge. I've heard a number of my women friends telling me about letting the air out of their ex-boyfriend's tires or writing their phone number on a bathroom wall. But even here, your deeper intention is to feel good even if your way to get there isn't particularly skillful.

If it's true for ourselves, it makes sense that it's true for other people. So I feel confident in saying that, most of the time when people do something hurtful, they are really just trying to meet their own needs. Sometimes the way the person went about meeting their needs was unskillful but they weren't trying to hurt us. A good test of this is to ask the other person or yourself, if I could have this need met and the person I hurt could actually feel good, would I prefer that?

These stories that we tell ourselves might be pretty harmless if we didn't allow them to get in the way of our lives. Unfortunately, there are two major downsides to holding onto them. The first is that they limit our capacity to choose new actions in the future with the person we feel has wronged us. If this is a person who doesn't really figure into your life in a major way then it may be no big deal. But what if it's your ex-spouse and you need to continue to make decisions about your children together?

The second disadvantage to these stories is that we tend to lump them together and generalize. Generalization is a way that humans make sense of lots of different actions so that we can make quick decisions. So if you have had three men in your life who have hurt you, particularly if you were dating them, you might generalize this experience to, "Men are bad. Or, "no man will ever love me the way I need." These stories can get in the way of what you actually would like to invite into your life.

I saw this clearly in a client I recently was in conversation with. I was suggesting that we might do some hypnosis or guided visualization exercises to help her through a block that she was experiencing. She had a strong reaction to this type of work which was interesting because she had many times expressed how much she trusted me. (This is the biggest obstacle to doing hypnosis with most clients.) When we talked more she told me that twenty two years ago she had been in a workshop where the person who was leading the guided meditation left her in a place she didn't want to be. She had generalized that one experience to all guided meditation and significantly decreased her options in the work we could do together.

So allowing ourselves to see our stories as our own constructions, but only after allowing ourselves to experience the emotions, allows us to move into a relationship with more choices. This can be either new relationships with other people or reformed versions of the relationships we have been in previously where we have been hurt.

Choose a new path

There are two main steps to letting go of old stories and living with more choices. The first is to tell a new story where you get to play the hero. And the second is to decide what actions make sense based on your new understandings and take them.

One of the best things about stories is that they are incredibly malleable. We can easily tell a story from a different angle or perspective. We do this naturally when we share our experiences with other people. Even when we tell people about a movie that we saw or a book that we read, it is filtered through our own perspective.

For most people, the story that they tell that gets them stuck is one of being a victim. How many times has someone said to you, "You'll never believe what _____ did to me?" We already know that blank didn't really do it to you the way you think he or she might have. But on top of that, you made some choices in the interaction as well.

One of the most fun options is to decide what you can actually learn from the incident and allow yourself to be the hero in the story. You can be the one who gained valuable insight or choose a new direction. Let me give you an example.

A friend was recently telling me what a jerk her boyfriend is. He seems, at least in her perspective, to be doing things that just don't meet her expectations. And then her feelings get hurt. He just doesn't understand her.

She can surely tell this story to everyone that she knows and she may very well get lots of sympathy. She has been so victimized by this relationship. What a saint she must be to stay. Of course, martyrs tend not to enjoy life very much so if her objective is joy than this strategy won't get her what she wants.

Perhaps a better alternative would be for her to determine what her actual needs are and imagine the myriad of ways that she could meet them. This might include telling her boyfriend what she would like from him. Or she might choose to meet some of her needs on her own or with the aid of friends. And she might even decide that she doesn't want to stay with him. If this happens, the story she gets to tell is how much she learned about herself in this relationship and how much more prepared she is to find a more appropriate partner.

So the two things that we just suggested are for her to take responsibility for her needs and see if she can meet them. She might be surprised that her boyfriend can meet her needs. She might also be surprised that her boyfriend probably had some needs of his own that are going unmet. Meeting his needs might make more space for a better relationship. No matter what happens she has taken responsibility for her experience and made choices for herself.

Initially, it may be difficult to release old stories. We have set up neural networks where the offender becomes a trigger for pain. This is particularly true when we have repeated interactions with someone that are negative. In order to really release the story at an emotional level, you will have to retrain the neural pathways.

One way to do this is by using the compassion meditation that you learned earlier in the book. Start moving compassion towards them not for the wrong they did you but for how scared, broken and unskilled they were. I find it helpful to do this meditation while focusing on the person as a little child, the scared part of themselves that they were likely acting out of when they hurt you. Remember, this is not for them. It's for you. We practice compassion for those that harmed us so they we can release our attachment to the anger. In the process, we heal parts of ourselves that we have kept hidden from sight because we thought they were unworthy of compassion and forgiveness.

The easiest to shift will be those that are the freshest in your mind. Those that you have had the least amount of time to rehearse your grievance story. Give yourself time. Each time you do this practice and you call to mind their face with compassion, you will ease the pain that you continue to carry.

You may find yourself triggered by mention of them even while you are working on this process. If that happens, practice simply stopping yourself and taking ten deep breaths with the meditation we learned earlier, "Breathing in I calm my body, breathing out I smile." Each time you practice this response, you will retrain your brain to have a calm reaction to hearing the person's name.

Take a few minutes now to think of all the people that you are holding onto past hurts with. Make a list of them. The idea here isn't to get hung up and spend a bunch of time stewing on what they did to you. It's just to see where you may want to practice forgiveness. Remember each one of these old grievances is hurting you more than the person you're angry with. Each one is blocking a part of your heart that could allow for more love in your life.

Now continue this by making a list of anything that you need to forgive yourself for. Perhaps you have done things that you are not proud of, broken commitments to yourself, acted out of alignment with your values. You may have acted unskillfully in trying to meet your needs and hurt people that you love or created bad situations for yourself. None of us is perfect. We all have places where we could offer ourselves forgiveness.

This is a good place to let go of any notions that you are carrying of yourself as a bad parent. It may be that you have to ask for forgiveness from your children. This is powerful example for them. We are all perfect in our imperfection but not if we pretend that we don't make mistakes. Unless you are willing to forgive yourself and to apologize, you will never be able to fully forgive your children for their imperfections.

Finally, make a list of all the places in your life where you are holding onto a wrong that you have committed against someone else. Can you see how asking for their forgiveness may create space for you both to be in fuller relationship?

Since many of us hide from our pain, allowing these feelings to arise can feel really big. Here are a few things you can keep in mind. It's helpful to acknowledge that dealing with the spaces in our lives where we have hurt others and they have hurt us can bring up lots of emotions. We might feel sad or angry, ashamed or embarrassed. Regardless of the emotion, you can know that you are bigger than it and simply let yourself experience it. Remember, allowing yourself to experience an emotion is different than becoming attached to it. Just let it pass through you like watching a cloud pass overhead.

When we are able to release these past hurts, we open a whole new territory in ourselves. It's like turning an old junkyard into a beautiful meadow where we are at last free to run and play without fear of tripping over hidden debris. Wouldn't you rather be carrying inside you a meadow than a junkyard?

Teach your children the three simple steps of forgiveness and talk to them about the importance of forgiving other people and themselves. As they learn this skill from you, both by what you teach them and what they see you do in your life, they will be able to live lighter lives with much less emotional real estate being taken over by past hurts. This leaves greater room for love and compassion to spill over into their lives!

Affirmation

Holding old grievances chain us to the past and limit our capacity to move forward with freedom and confidence into our future. Say ten times, "I am freely releasing all past hurts. They are evicted from my mind, my heart and my body!"

Self-Observation

For the next week notice how you hold onto past grievances. Notice how this affects your current actions. Write down your observations in your journal.

Practice

You don't have to forgive anyone ever. It is your choice. When you are ready to let go of past pain, the process is available to you. See if there are people in your life that you are ready to forgive. You can even practice with people who have made very small infractions, such as cutting you off in traffic or taking the last melon at the market, the one you really wanted. Go through the process explained in the chapter. Note in your journal how you felt moving through this process.

Chapter 25: Make Friends with Anger

Do not teach your children never to be angry; teach them how to be angry.

~ Lyman Abbott

Holding on to anger is like grasping a hot coal with the intent of throwing it at someone else; you are the one who gets burned.
~Buddha

Many of us have had the experience of growing up with a very angry parent. For me, my father seemed to always be mad at the world. He would fly into violent screaming fits that were completely unpredictable. I learned to be quiet, stay in the background as much as possible and try not to provoke anything. But when nothing big was present, smaller things like an unwashed glass in the sink would become the trigger.

Trying to be in relationship with someone with this level of anger is almost impossible. Even a simple conversation can feel like walking through a minefield where you are never certain where the next explosion will come from. The message I received very early was that anger was a dangerous emotion that needed to be controlled at all costs.

Unfortunately, my father was acting out deeply embedded cultural patterns. Men are allowed to show anger and discouraged from exhibiting softer emotions. I am happy that this has softened a bit since I was a child but these stereotypes still exist.

For young women, the opposite tends to be true. They are often encouraged to hide their anger and only reveal their softer side. To be "sugar and spice and everything nice." This can lead young women into depression as well as other disorders where their emotions get suppressed. Neither strategy serves us very well. We end up with men who are all too comfortable with violence and rage and women who are incapable of owning their needs and drawing strong boundaries.

It took me years to understand that my father's anger grew out of his pain and his brokenness. It was hard to admit that he was not a bad man but just very unskillful in the way that he expressed his emotions. The more I was able to do this, the more I have been able to call back into myself the rightful place of anger in the emotional repertoire.

You may have noticed that, as you have engaged in the practices up to this point, your level of anger has naturally decreased. You have been meeting your needs, releasing your expectations, forgiving past hurts, all things that tie us to anger that isn't in the present and giving us more space to deal with the anger we might feel now. These practices offer a re-balancing returning anger to its rightful place that, at certain points, has an important part to play in our lives.

Some people think that by walking down a spiritual path, one gives up strong emotion. You must let go of anger and lust and pride. But there is nothing wrong with anger. And the spiritual path is learning primarily to be with what is. The real learning here is how to befriend your anger so it becomes an ally instead of your worst enemy. Anger can be very valuable when it's channeled.

Anger is a warning system that tells you something is not right. Your needs or those around you are not being met. Some have mistakenly called this an early warning system but this isn't quite right. Emotional awareness is really the early warning system which is part of why we encourage meditation and awareness practice with all of our clients. Simple awareness creates more space to notice the things, which left unmet, will eventually make us angry. Think of it this way. Imagine if you stepped on a small splinter. If you are really connected to your body you might feel it, say ouch and move to address it. If you miss it, the splinter might slowly work its way into your system till it causes some significant pain and then you really start to feel it. OUCH! This is anger.

So when we experience anger, we can realize that it is telling us that something isn't right in our world. And then we begin to be able to pay attention to what that might be. Here we simply return to seeing what is right in front of us and take the time to ask what is really going on. Often when we experience anger we want to discharge it so quickly that we don't have the time to understand what it is trying to teach us. We have all probably had times when we have acted too quickly from an angry place and made a decision that wasn't the wisest thing we could do. If we can simply stay with the anger without dwelling in its attached story, we can often find deeper truth lies within it.

Imagine that you just found out that your child has been smoking after school with some friends. You might get very angry with them. You taught them better than that (much more of a statement about you than their decision), you don't want to see them damage their health (concern), and what else might these friends lead them into (fear)? In just this one example all kinds of stories and emotions are tied to the anger. Some of it is may be about your own sense of pride being hurt or even feeling like you have been defied. But the higher purpose is your concern for the wellbeing and safety of your child.

If you were to choose to act out of anger in this situation you might send your child off to their room to think about what they did or scream and yell at them. You might tell them that you can't believe what bad choices they are making and you are really disappointed. However, none of this helps you to connect with your child, protect their health and help them to make wiser decisions. Your higher intention would be much better served in waiting until you have had the time to calm down and then express your true concern. If there are to be consequences that go along with their actions, this will also help you have the time to think about what is appropriate in that regard.

And when you do yell and scream, or "lose it", because your son or daughter has done something that you just can't believe, it is important that you go back to the place of forgiveness. First forgive yourself for not acting skillfully and forgive your child for making choices that you disagree with. And ask your children for forgiveness for the way that you acted. You might even forgive the friends who have been involved in these choices so that you are able to have a much wider influence. Anger is a potent force that can be difficult to control once it rears its head. Few us were raised with the skills to deal with it. So simply forgive yourself and come back to where you would like to be in your parenting.

If your anger seems to come up around a particular trigger, so that there is a pattern, it may be that you want to widen the scope of your "anger dialogue." If every time things don't go your way, you scream and shout, eventually sorry may not be enough. Part of genuine apology is seeking ways to shift the behavior. So if you do find that something in particular pushes you over the edge, see if you can identify its source. Using the tools that you have been learning throughout this book, consider the following:

- Is there a particular story that you are telling about this action? For example, your child doesn't do what you say because they don't respect you.

- Ask yourself if this is really a projection of your own. So if you think your child isn't respecting you, ask yourself if that's something that's coming up in other areas of your life. Or maybe it reminds you of something one of your parents always did to you. In fact, you may not be respecting yourself or others in your life very much and you may ask yourself how that behavior is reflected in your own life.

- Ask yourself if you are getting what you want from your behavior? What is your higher purpose in these outbursts? See if you can see how these displays of great force can often be counterproductive to your children really listening to you.

- Consider that you may want to get help from a coach or therapist that does work with anger management. If you have learned unhealthy patterns of dealing with anger, you will likely pass those on to your children. Ask yourself if that is really the legacy that you want to pass on to them and, if not, what are you willing to do to change? One of the most powerful things that you can do is ask for help!

Affirmation

Anger helps us to know when things are out of balance. It can be a great teaching tool that leads to wisdom that we did not expect. In order to mine that anger for its wisdom, we must allow it to communicate at the deepest levels. This week, practice affirming the phrase, "I am allowing my anger to teach me what it will. I patiently wait to act on my anger until I am truly prepared.

Self-Observation

Notice how often you get angry throughout your day? How do you feel after you get angry? See if there is a story behind your anger. What is it trying to show you? Record your observations in your journal.

Practice

Sometimes when we follow our anger, we see that it's simply old patterns that are expressing themselves. In those cases, shifting the story around that situation is one of the most powerful things we can do. But often our anger is telling us that something is not right. Where you see that your anger is telling you something is really not right, ask yourself what your highest intention is with this circumstance and what you would rather see happen? Then take the time to imagine what options might get you there. Use all of the tools that you have learned throughout this book to expand your options. And then try out one of these actions. Feel free to start small at first!

Chapter 26: Laugh Out Loud

At the height of laughter, the universe is flung into a kaleidoscope of new possibilities.

~Jean Houston

Laughter is the shortest distance between two people.

~Victor Borge

Dad always thought laughter was the best medicine, which I guess is why several of us died of tuberculosis.

~Jack Handey, "Deep Thoughts," Saturday Night Live

One of the truest fruits of joy is laughter. When we are able to be touched at our deepest levels, to laugh at ourselves and to laugh with others we experience greater health, deeper connections and increased peace of mind. If there was one powerful practice that we could leave you with, it would be simply to adopt a laughter habit. Choose to laugh everyday. You can do this with the aid of funny materials like movies or jokes or you can adopt a practice of laughter yoga.

My grandmother Edie taught me more about laughter than just about any person in my life. She was always laughing at something. One day she called me to tell me that she had decided what songs that she would like played at her funeral. I was expecting this might be serious as she had been worried about her health after my grandfather died. She proceeded to tell me that she would like, "Don't Step on My Tutu" and started laughing. Eventually we decided that the funeral would not be complete without also playing "Grandma Got Run Over by a Reindeer." Even in the face of death we can choose to laugh and enjoy life.

Families that are able to laugh together express a deep, enduring bond. They share a comfort and connection with each other that endures throughout the good times and the bad times. And it's one of our favorite things to see in families. It's particularly powerful when we come to a place that we are able to laugh at our own foibles as we embrace new possibilities.

As important as this is, you would think that more families would think of ways that they can laugh together. You would expect them to be going off to laughter camps and practice the deep belly laughing that calms the body and the mind. And yet very few people have done this. In part, this is because we have been convinced that laughter starts outside of ourselves.

However, a number of years ago, a doctor in India named Madan Kateria realized the amazing power of laughter in healing. He started seeking out jokes that he could tell his patients. Eventually, he realized that his patients could actually learn to laugh without any stimulus. They didn't need jokes or funny movies or even whoopee cushions. If they simply performed the same actions as laughter, the same healing effects came about. In response, he and his wife started laughter clubs where people get together and practice laughing. These clubs have now spread all over the world.

You can take up Dr. Kateria's mantle and simply go into a closed room and practice laughing. This has amazing physiological effects. Your breathing will deepen, you will feel calmer and your mind will be more relaxed and expansive. You can also gather together funny movies, find jokes that you love and books or cartoons that make you giggle. Having a laughter first aid kit is often some of the best medicine you can take under stress.

In your family, simply begin to pay attention to how much you are laughing together. As in all things, the laughter should not be at the expense of a family member as this will work against your highest intention of being more connected and loving. If you notice that your family is not laughing much, consider spending more time renting funny movies and playing silly games. Take notice of what it is that makes your children and your spouse laugh and bring more of that to the family. And be an example for your children, we all know how contagious laughter can be. What better thing to spread?

Affirmation

It's hard to stay mad when we are laughing. In fact, all of our troubles seem to fade away and we come into the present moment without even trying. Use the following affirmation to celebrate the power of laughter and mirth in your life. "Today I celebrate joy and laughter. I will allow myself to laugh wherever the universe provides the humor."

Self-Observation

For the next week notice how often you laugh. What about your family? Your co-workers? Notice if you are in environments that promote levity and humor. How does it feel to be in these environments?

Practice

Since you've come all the way to the end of the book and haven't rebelled, we thought we would give you this practice as a reward. This week, simply practice laughing out loud. You can think of something funny if you need it to get you started but then simply practicing bringing up great big belly laughs anytime you want. Do this everyday for five minutes and notice how you feel afterwards. Warning: We don't recommend doing this in on the subway or atthe mall. ☺

Afterward

"We shall not cease from exploration, and the end of all our exploring will be to arrive where we started and know the place for the first time."

~ T. S. Eliot

When I first told my mother that Dan and I were writing a book about parenting she asked, with some concern in her voice, "if I was going to talk about all the things that she did wrong." We laughed even as I convinced her that she was not the subject of a "Mommy Dearest" expose.

Of course, my parents were not perfect. They did the best they could with the resources that they had. And that's all that anyone can do. No one will be the best parent, partner, friend, employee or child. So we learn to become more skillful where we can and ask forgiveness where we miss the mark.

Dan and I are honored that you have gone through this journey of our ideas and practices that we know have the potential to help you because we have seen them work. We have seen them change the lives of people that we have coached and counseled. This is a journey back to yourself, to awakening to all that is your birthright. But be gentle with yourself. The work is fun and rewarding if you allow it to be.

You may find, once you have gotten to the end of this work, that you want to work with it on a deeper level. This can be done in a number of ways. You may gather a small group in your community and explore how these concepts play out in the lives of other parents. You might explore how they spill over into the rest of your life. Or you may decide that you want to work with a coach to help you gain greater understanding and skillfullness in using these practices.

For many people coaching can help them increase the value of this work exponentially. In part, this is because coaches can see outside of the lenses that you have. Often a client begins a practice only to have it open up entirely with just a little adjustment from the coach. For example, some people go about practicing the concept of effortless effort with extreme effort. That's how they've done their lives. They make lists and plan. Helping them see how different a concept this is can really make a difference. Coaching also gives you an opportunity for support that we don't experience very many places in our lives.

If you would like to explore coaching with one of us, Dan and I are both happy to talk with you or you can find more information on our websites listed in the about the authors sections. You may also be interested in attending one of the workshops that we lead.

We believe in this work because we see it work daily and we would be excited to assist you in finding more fulfilling ways to be in relationship to yourself and your children. No matter how you may choose to continue with this work, we know that simply by reading and reflecting on these ideas, you will be able to bring new perspective in relating to your children. We wish you and your families all the best on your journey!

About the Authors

Dr. Scott Mills, Ph.D. is an expert in human change, development and achievement coaching individuals and organizations in the U.S. and Canada. He is focused on how to make the world more livable, more full of love and passion, and more capable of compassion. He has a particular love for working with youth and families. He holds a Ph.D. in Religion and Psychology and is a Certified Integral Coach. Most important, he laughs often, loves his work and couldn't imagine a better life.

He is very open to talking with you about your hopes and dreams, your goals in life and the way that he can help you achieve them. If you would like to find out more about him, or are interested in coaching, please visit his website at www.joyandbalance.com.

Dr. Dan Kaufman, Ed.D. holds a strong commitment to himself and to those that he works with to being fully present, connecting compassionately and helping families and individuals find within themselves a deep sense of peace and purpose in their lives. He has a deep respect and compassion for adolescents and parents and believes that helping them to be more loving, caring, and understanding of one another plants the seeds for a more peaceful and compassionate world. His own compassion for others helps create a deep sense of trust between himself and those that he works with and is a foundation for change.

He holds a Doctorate in Education, completed doctoral level work in Counseling Psychology, holds a Master's degree in Psychology and is a Certified Integral Coach and Licensed Mental Health Counselor.

He is passionate about his work and invites you to contact him if you would like to learn more about him, his work and how he can help support significant changes in your life. To learn more about him you can visit his website www.spiraltohealth.com or contact him at dan@spiraltohealth.com.

Your Stories

We are always excited and enriched by hearing the stories of parents we have worked with, who have read our work and who have such valuable insight to offer. We would love to hear your feedback, ideas, and anecdotes about how these ideas have affected your journey! Please share them with us at stories@joyandandbalance.com.

Further Resources

Additional resources, articles, and CDs are available at www.joyandbalance.com. We encourage you to visit the website often as new resources are added frequently.

We are very proud to offer a series of hypnosis CDs designed to accompany this book. If you enjoy guided practices that will assist you in moving forward with even greater ease and support, we encourage you to check these out on the website!

Drs. Scott Mills and Dan Kaufman

www.ingramcontent.com/pod-product-compliance
Lightning Source LLC
Chambersburg PA
CBHW021101090426
42738CB00006B/453